HEY
Just a Kid
(a True Story)

Ron Bond

outskirtspress
DENVER, COLORADO

Outskirts Press, Inc.
http://www.outskirtspress.com

ISBN: 978-1-4327-8821-6

Outskirts Press and the "OP" logo are trademarks belonging to Outskirts Press, Inc.

PRINTED IN THE UNITED STATES OF AMERICA

Special thanks to my lovely wife Jeanette for reading each one of my stories and saying, "Now I know why you are the way you are!" To my friends Regina Scammon and Kevin Dowling for editing, content review, and laughs along the way. Front cover by jmbdesignsli.webs.com.

Table of Contents

School's Out

IT WAS ALMOST three o'clock on a school day. Even though I didn't look at the clock on the wall, I knew the school day is almost over when the teacher wrote tonight's homework on the blackboard. The early dismissal bell rang, and the bused-in kids like me got up out of our chairs and left the classroom early. Six long yellow buses waited outside for us. We sat two kids on each side, on green bench seats with windows on each side of the bus. On the ride home, I usually sat with the same kids, and sometimes a friend would save a seat for me. After the bus stopped in different neighborhoods, dropping off kids, the school bus drove down Morris Park Avenue, until we reached my stop, Tremont and Morris Park Avenue. Most kids that got off the bus were met by someone — a mother, a father, a big brother or sister. No one was ever there to meet me.

I walked down the block toward my building on 437 Morris Park Avenue. On the way home, I walked past Dunrite Movers, and the neighborhood bar, where I poked my head in to see if Mom was there. Today she wasn't there. Then came Harry's candy store on the corner of Morris Park and Lebanon Street. I walked to my building and ran up the staircase to the fourth floor to my apartment. I ran up two steps at a time, while holding on to the banister with my left hand and books in my right hand. I pretended that each step was on fire, so I barely touched down before I was on the next step. Flights of stairs go fast when you take them two at a time and make a game of it.

My apartment door was still open from this morning when I left for school. Since I didn't see Mom at the bar when I looked in, I knew she was still sleeping, so I entered the apartment quietly. I heard her snoring in the bedroom; she was asleep, just the way I left her. By the bed on the night table, the plastic top was off her coffee cup, and it wasn't full anymore. The French cruller that I bought this morning with the coffee and cigarettes was bit into. It was shaped like a half moon now instead of a circle. The Kool Kings 100s pack of cigarettes was open, and three cigarette butts were smashed into the black plastic ashtray. She had probably been up and awake for about twenty minutes, judging by the coffee that was now half-drunk. Every day was the same with her. If she wasn't in the bar when I walked by, that meant she never got up and out of the house, so I would find her home still asleep.

I walked down the hall into the living room and watched television. I drifted between Channel 5, Channel 9, or Channel 11. Those were my favorite channels to watch. On those channels I watched Superman, Abbott and Costello, The Three Stooges, Bugs Bunny and Daffy Duck cartoons, Popeye, and Felix the Cat. After a few hours of watching television I got hungry, and since Mom didn't cook and wasn't awake, and there was no food in the refrigerator, I left the apartment and went downstairs to Harry's candy store and luncheonette. Harry's was the center of the whole neighborhood.

After I passed Johnny Moon, the tense, tough-guy teenager who stood guard at the front of the door, I walked into Harry's. Once inside, Harry and his whole family were there. Behind the counter were Harry, his wife Florence, his older pretty daughter Barbara, and big Alice, who was a few years older than me. She usually sat at the last red stool at the counter with a bunch of French fries in front of her, reading a magazine. Harry's had everything; you could get candy and ice cream, newspapers and magazines, and toys. There was a soda fountain with hand-pumped syrups that flavored seltzer water that came out of the long silver spigot with the black handle. At Harry's, there was also a grill for hamburgers and hotdogs and grilled cheese sandwiches. Everything came with a pickle and French fries. A more complete meal a kid could never find.

The last six seats at the counter were for food; the others were for fountain sodas and ice cream. While you waited for food or a soda, there were comic books in a rack by the window. If it was busy enough, you could finish a few comic books without actually buying them. It was easy to keep up with Superman and Batman and Archie, while Harry and Florence were cooking behind the counter. Near the door was a red Coca-Cola cold soda box that opened on the top with two sliders. The left side was soda floating in ice and water that froze your fingertips by the time you pulled out your favorite soda. The right slider had ices and ice cream packed neatly to the top, like bricks in a wall. Next to that was a telephone booth with an accordion door that closed, to give you privacy when you spoke.

I ordered a Coke, burger, and fries. Florence reached into the freezer and came out with a frozen burger patty that she put on the hot grill. Then she put the frozen French fries into the hot oil basket. They made a bubbling sound as they cooked. The Wurlitzer jukebox near the telephone booth was playing "Sugar Shack," and if there was a quarter put in there, there would be two more songs after that. As soon as the burger and fries were done and placed in front of me, before the Coke was poured, Florence asked me if I wanted a splash of vanilla or cherry squirted into the Coke for a nickel more. Tonight, it was one vanilla pump from the nozzle to sweeten up the Coke.

As I ate the burger and listened to music, I waited for my father to come into Harry's like he always did before he went up to the apartment. He usually came into Harry's around five or five-thirty, when he got off the train. He stopped at Harry's every night after work, sometimes to borrow money for the next day, or to place a bet on a horse race at Belmont or Roosevelt Racetrack. Then, he would ask Harry for the winning numbers of the day that he played the night before. Harry and that luncheonette ran everything on our block. Harry was a tall, thin man with short gray hair, cut military style, and he walked with a limp on his left leg.

The story that was told on our block that he got his limp from being shot in the leg when he was a young man, and had been a gangster. He told everyone he was a button man for Dutch Schultz. I don't know what a button man was, but I knew what a gangster was. On Saturday afternoons when I slept over at my Nanny's house, I watched James Cagney movies with her. After she cleaned the house, she would always ask me if I wanted to watch old gangster movies with her. She seemed to enjoy them so much that I could never refuse her. It must have been true about Harry being a gangster, because all day long tough-looking guys like in the movies, about Harry's age, would come into the candy store to visit with him. They sat in the back and drank coffee with Harry, and they told stories. At the end of the stories they would laugh and pat each other on the back, and fold their fingers in their hand to make them look like a gun, and they would pretend to shoot each other while they laughed. I saw many of these men hand money to Harry all during the day. I was just a kid, so while I didn't know what Harry did, all I know was that he had a great candy store. All the rest was over my head, and it was probably better that way. Sometimes, knowing someone's past makes you see them differently.

Harry knew all the kids, and all of our names, but when you spoke to him, he just stared at you when we went into his candy store, like he didn't know us, and would ask, "What do you want, kid?" He never called you by name; we were all just kids to him. He had a way of keeping us quiet and keeping us kids in line just by being himself. Maybe it was his size, or the gray hair, or his deep blue eyes that didn't blink as he stared at you. When he locked eyes on you in his store, you would always behave. Because of who he was on the block, and what he gave us, we all felt grateful to him and his candy store.

My father told me that Harry was what you call a loan shark (maybe that explained his cold, lifeless eyes). He said Harry would loan you money, and when it was paid back, he made you give him back more money than the money he gave you. The longer you owed, the more you had to pay back. My dad also said Harry was a bookie. I never got the explanation on bookie, and how it all worked. By own-ing the candy store and the other things he did, Harry was the rich guy in the neighborhood, and he lived down the block on Lebanon Street in The Bronx, the same neighborhood with all of us. Harry knew I was Buster's kid, so I could always go there for food or candy, anytime I wanted, and I could even have a small toy that was on the counter — but never the ones that were in the big glass case in the back of the store.

On the night I'm telling you about, Dad came in and saw me at the counter. He went to Harry first, and whispered something to Harry. Then Harry put his hand in his pocket and pulled out a big roll of money wrapped in a rubber band. He handed my father twenty dollars. Dad said, "I'll see you Friday, Harry." He put the money in his pocket as he walked over and patted me on the head. He never kissed me in public, and hardly talked to me. He saw my paper plate had only a few fries left, and he motioned to me with his arm. That meant *Let's go.*

We walked to our building to go up to the apartment. When I was with him, we took the elevator; when I was alone, I always took the stairs. I could run up four flights of stairs before any elevator would arrive at the lobby, so why wait? We got out on the fourth floor and walked down the hall to our apartment. He went left to the bedroom. I went to the right, to the living room, and turned on the television, so I could watch cartoons and do homework at the same time. Before the television had a chance to come on, the screaming started. For a quiet man, his voice surrounded the apartment as he yelled at Mom. For a woman who was sleeping a moment ago, her voice was louder than the television that I sat in front of. After working as a laborer all day, finding Mom still in bed, a dirty house, no dinner, what else could he do?

After an hour of fighting, Dad got into the shower and got dressed to leave for the night. By the time the apartment door closed behind him, Mom was in the shower and ready to start her night. Sometimes she remembered to lock me in; other times after I did homework, before I went to bed, I locked the door. Neither of them ever said goodbye to me. Almost every day and every night was like this. There were no milk and cookies before bed, no mom to tuck me in, no kiss on the forehead like on *Leave It to Beaver* or *Lassie*. With them both out of the house it was quiet now, and I was tired. It was bedtime. I crawled into my bed that was waiting there for me. It was exactly how I left it that morning. The big blanket Nanny gave me for Christmas was crumpled up at the bottom of the bed. I pulled it up over my shoulders and wiggled my head into the pillow until it was just right. I whispered the nighttime prayer that Nanny taught me, closed my eyes, and smiled, thinking about tomorrow and what I was going to do in school.

Nanny's House

CROSBY AVENUE, IN The Bronx, where Nanny lived, was truly an exciting place. The avenue had every store imaginable. There were two clothing stores, a hardware store, four candy stores, a drugstore, two bakeries, a supermarket, three pizza places, a florist, a butcher, an Italian specialty store called a "Latticini," two banks, a card store, a bar on every corner, a tailor, a hobby shop for kids — even a funeral parlor, so you could live and die right on the same block, without ever leaving the neighborhood. It was like a complete city on her block. People who lived in the area didn't have to venture far to find anything and everything they needed. The neighborhood grew out of convenience. There was a train station on Crosby and Buhre Avenue, so anyone who worked in Manhattan, Queens, or Brooklyn had to walk along that street. All of the neighborhood people shopped there; you never had to leave the block for anything.

Nanny and Granddad lived in a small apartment building on Crosby Avenue. Before you entered the hallway of the building, to the left was a barber shop, to the right a tailor shop, and next to the tailor shop was a bar. Once inside the building, you came face-to-face with a mountain of marble steps and wrought-iron banisters with wooden handrails. In the winter the halls were always warm. The steam radiators hissed as heat was pumped throughout the building from a coal furnace in the basement. Nanny lived on the third floor. Since there were so many stairs, I would make a game out of climbing them. I pretended that the banister was a vine, and the stairs a steep mountain, and I pulled myself up each step hand over hand until I got to the top of each landing.

Nanny's building was not like mine; it was very quiet, and you could tell no kids lived there. The last group of kids that lived there were my father and my aunts, when the building was new about twenty-five years ago. Usually, I was the only kid in the building, and I was just visiting. When I reached the first landing, I counted the doors: there were four apartments on each floor. On this floor I could smell the aroma of some food cooking, but I couldn't identify it. Nanny always told me to be very quiet when I climbed up the stairs to her apartment. "Don't make any noise; you'll get in trouble," she said. She told me that on that floor was a big German lady named Mrs. Wieberg. Even though they lived in the same building, Nanny didn't know her first name, and they never spoke to each other. She told me that if I made noise, Mrs. Wieberg would open the door and yell at me. Whether that was true or not, the threat was enough to keep me quiet. I had to climb another flight of stairs, so I continued to play Tarzan, and the banister was my vine.

Once I reached Nanny's floor, I could smell more food cooking. It was a familiar sweet aroma of Italian food that I enjoyed so much. All the ladies on Nanny's floor were Italian. There were Mrs. Greco, Mrs. Squitari, and Jimmy Cigar's wife — I never knew her name or saw her, but I knew old man Jimmy lived there and he always smoked a cigar, so everybody called him Jimmy Cigar. I guess it is a stereotype, but it is true that all Italian women love to cook. Maybe they don't love it, but they cook anyway, and the smell of food on that floor made me hungry by the time I reached the top of the vine.

To the right was apartment number seven, Nanny's house. Everyone who lived in an apartment called it a house. When I watched TV, the houses looked like real houses with grass and trees, and a car in the driveway, not like apartments in buildings. This was The Bronx, not TV land. On Nanny's apartment door, there was no bell to ring. There was a big brass metal doorknocker shaped like a horseshoe. I had to stand on my toes to reach it. When I knocked, I used our family's signature knock: five rapid knocks, a pause, then two more. This was also the way my grandfather and father blew the car horn. I always thought the timing of that knock and car horn beep was invented by my grandfather, since he was a musician and had some rhythm. I once asked him about the knock. He told me it meant "shave and a haircut ... two bits." I never knew what that meant, but it must have meant something to him and the rest of my family, since everybody used it.

When I was done with the knock, the door opened magically. There she was, my Nanny. She would scoop me up in her soft round arms like I was a soldier coming home from the war, like she hadn't seen me in such a long time — that's how she greeted me; you could feel our love through the squeeze. Once inside the apartment, you could hear the food cooking. On her little gas stove was a big frying pan of hot oil popping, frying up the meatballs. The television in the living room was blasting very loud; Granddad was a little bit hard of hearing, so the volume was cranked up. There she stood, less than five feet tall and about three feet wide, her shy sincere smile on her soft pink lips. Her eyes were dark brown, almost black, with no visible pupils, like a doll's eyes. She always wore a flowered dress with a colorful flowered cooking apron to match. Above her eyes were perfectly pencil-drawn brown eyebrows. Her hair was thin and her bangs were cut and curled a half inch above her eyebrows, framing her face like a photograph. On top of her thinning hair was a curly thick nest of a wig that her bangs popped out of. She looked dressed up, and she wore gold earrings with a big pearl in the middle. The pearl was cut in half and lay in the center of the earring, so it probably wasn't a real pearl, but she made them look precious.

Once inside the apartment, the door got locked behind me. I shot a glance at the mirror in the hall that was strategically placed on the wall. Nanny and Granddad could watch each other as he read *The Daily News* and watched TV while Nanny cooked in the kitchen. Granddad sat on the old blue and green paisley sofa. He wore black dress pants with black leather slippers and black silk socks that rested on a foot rest that didn't match the furniture. He had his legs crossed at the bottom by his ankles. His hands were so big; the newspaper looked like a comic book as he held it. He wore a blue silk quilted smoking jacket with maroon collar and cuffs. He had a red paisley ascot tied neatly around his neck. Granddad looked like a silent screen movie actor. His dyed black hair was slicked back and held in place by a gold tube of V-05 that he kept in the medicine cabinet. He held his head high and his posture stiff as if cameras were in the room ready to photograph him. I, too, thought he was an old movie star. I looked for the mantelpiece above the fireplace for the Oscars, but there was no fireplace, and no Oscars. This was a third-floor walk-up apartment in The Bronx, but to look at Granddad you would never know it.

Nanny would gently move me into the kitchen. I don't remember walking; it was like she lifted me up and sat me down in front of Nabisco Golden Wafers and a glass of milk. The dishes were soaking in the sink; the food was frying on the stove. When the cookies were gone, she walked me to the bathroom down the hall and ran the bathwater. While I was taking a bath, Nanny gathered my dirty clothes and put them in the washing machine. After the bath, I was given pajamas and had dinner with Nanny and Granddad. Nanny would always do all the work; Granddad never offered to help, because he already worked that day and now he was home. Nanny's job never ended; she was never off. Nanny served Granddad first, then me, then she sat last, after everything was placed on the table. Her eyes were always on me, with a big smile, like I was some kind of prize. Granddad sat at the kitchen table and told stories about himself and all his accomplishments.

At seven years old, I didn't really know what Granddad did. I know when I slept over I had to sleep in his room — not in their bedroom where they slept, but in his room. When you entered Granddad's room, to the left there were lots of Army uniforms layered one on top of the other, with Army medals pinned on the uniforms and on the wall. There were two rifles hanging barrel up next to each other. On the same wall there was a giant black-and-white picture of him holding his guitar. His hair was slicked back; he was wearing a white silk suit, white shirt, and a black silk bow tie. He had a confident open-mouthed broad smile, like someone just complimented him, and clicked his picture. That was Granddad's rehearsed smile, a movie star's smile.

Then came the fishing rods that hung on nails off the wood molding. Next to the fishing rods came the cowboy stuff, a big white trophy with a gold horse on top, with his initials on it, from "The L. B. Ranch." There were four cowboy hats: one white, one brown, one black, one tan. They were the kind of hats John Wayne wore in the cowboy movies. There were pictures of Granddad on horseback with gold and blue ribbons around the pictures, like he won some prizes for being a cowboy. Then near the door there was a small desk with drafting tools and plastering molds, music books, and boxes of pictures of Granddad. So by the time I woke up, I thought Granddad was a great military general, who owned a ranch, and he was a cowboy, and when he wasn't busy on the stage as a musician, he was a fisherman, and an architect building houses with all his tools and blueprints. At my age, I really didn't know what Granddad was. I never understood how one man could be all of these things, but somehow he was, and he loved telling stories to support every occupation that hung on the wall.

The room was dark and cold, and the couch bed that I slept on creaked with every movement. I usually got up very early, around six-thirty in the morning. Before the cartoons came on, I watched *Modern Farmer,* thinking I might learn something useful for my granddad's ranch. Nanny would wake up about the same time as me. She would look in on me, and then go right into the bathroom to clean and dress before Granddad woke up. She sat at the kitchen table next to an AM radio and listened to the news. She drank her coffee as she put on her face makeup in a small round magnifying mirror that sat on the table in front of her.

A few hours later, Granddad got up. While en route to the

bathroom, he whistled to Nanny to signal that he was up. Makeup done or not, Nanny had the task of getting breakfast ready before he came out of the bathroom. He wasn't good at waiting, since he was such an important man. Granddad always ate the same thing for breakfast: bacon and eggs, two pieces of buttered toast, a small glass of orange juice, and coffee. Nanny had just toast, and I joined them for cereal and milk. The day went by fast. I watched TV all day. Saturday was the best cartoon day, and *Wonderama* was on, with Sonny Fox as the host. Sonny was a grown man who liked cartoons as much as his audience did. This was too good to be true: Bugs Bunny, Popeye cartoons, and The Three Stooges all day long.

About four o'clock, Granddad turned off the TV and put on Guy Lombardo records, and danced around the house. Granddad, always the showman, danced around the house with his left arm out and his right arm holding an imaginary dance partner. He danced mechanically with the rhythm of a soldier as he danced in front of the mirror, watching himself as the music played. Every Saturday they went dancing at a place in Manhattan called Roseland. Also every Saturday, Nanny made steak and French fries for dinner. By six o'clock, I was in the old Chevy Biscayne being dropped off at my apartment, so they wouldn't miss the opening dance of Guy Lombardo's Orchestra, when he said, "Is everybody happy?" I closed the car door behind me, kissed Nanny and Granddad, and walked up the stairs. My clothes were clean. My belly was full, and Nanny gave me the love and attention no one else did.

When I opened the door, the apartment was empty, but it was okay, since I had such a great weekend at Nanny's house.

Johnny Moon

HE STOOD LIKE a palace guard in front of the candy store. He never spoke much. We all knew him as Johnny Moon. Johnny had long black slicked-back hair, and in the front, a dozen tight fusilli-pasta-like curls that stopped right before they went into his eyes. He wore black jeans that were so tight he didn't need the thick black leather belt that held them up. Johnny wore a black leather jacket and a black button-up silk shirt with the top three buttons open, so underneath you could see his white T-shirt and gold cross on a chain. His face was always tight like he was ready and angry enough for a fight. He rarely smiled, and when he did, you could see he had chipped front teeth that added to his tough-guy looks. On his belt loop was a thick silver chain, like the kind of chain used to walk a big dog. The chain was attached to a black leather wallet he kept in his front pocket. His back was always to the wall, with his right leg bent at the knee and touching the back wall with his black motorcycle boots on the out-side of the candy store wall.

Johnny didn't live in our neighborhood; we could see him get on and off the bus at the Morris Park and Tremont Avenue bus stop, and walk to Harry's candy store. After he ate his hamburger, fries, and soda he would take his post outside the candy store's brick wall next to the door. He was our tough guy on the corner. Johnny was probably eighteen or nineteen years old, and even though we had teenagers his age who lived on the block, he didn't play ball with them or hang out with them. When he saw them, he just nodded his head while they would say his name — "Johnny Moon" — while they passed him to get into the candy store. Everybody was afraid of Johnny Moon. We never saw him fight, but he looked tough, so he never had to prove himself. Everyone got quiet around him, fearful of his reaction to what you might say, which would set him off and he could turn on you and beat you down. There was never a day that you didn't see Johnny standing guard protecting the neighborhood. We all felt safe when Johnny was around; nobody from another block in The Bronx would come onto our block looking for trouble. Johnny set the 20-yard line boundary just by being there and looking tough.

Johnny had no gang; he didn't need one. He could stare anyone down and he never had to throw a punch. At night, around eleven o'clock when Harry closed the candy store, that's when Johnny would go home. They say that's how he got his name. He went home late after dark when the moon came out. His sentinel duty was over. Now the block was quiet. Everyone was in their apartments for the night. Come tomorrow, Johnny Moon would be back in front of the candy store, standing guard, Johnny ... he always came back. A soldier never leaves his post, and Johnny never left the front of Harry's candy store.

Egg on His Face

MY FATHER WAS too young to be a father. He became a father at eighteen years old. At eighteen, you are still a growing teenager yourself. So success at being a parent is a long shot. To be so young and take on a job, a wife, and the child is quite a humongous task. It's like climbing Mount Everest in sneakers wearing only a sweater. When I was around seven or eight years old, Dad was still a young man, twenty-five or so. Since I was conceived in the backseat of a Buick, planning was not my dad's strong point. In the 50s and 60s, children were more part of the household than the focus of a family. Kids remained in the background, especially if you were not born to wealth and privilege or educated parents. What Dad did possess was the power of youthful flexibility. One day he was a construction worker, the next a gambler, the next a singer for doo-wop group. Sometimes on weekends he was all these things in the same day. He faced all this while having a crazy, pill-popping, lazy wife who drank, and a child, (me) who needed to be raised. Being a child living with my kind of parents, I had a window into the adult world of crazy. A television sitcom called *Petticoat Junction* was very popular. We could have had our own sitcom called *Dysfunction Junction*.

Dad was a ruggedly handsome man, a well-built six footer. He had a Roman nose that fit his face and did not detract from his good looks. He had warm kind eyes, like his mother, my Nanny. Being a young, handsome man, Dad lived in the mirror. He adjusted his 50s hairdo and tossed the front so it looked casually windblown, even though each curl was placed with care on his forehead. Sometimes from the bathroom, after his hair was perfected, you could hear him practicing being a tough guy. He cranked out his jaw like a gangster and rehearsed. "What are you looking at? I'll break your ass! Oh yeah, and I'll put you in the hospital." When I heard this, and walked in on him, he was never embarrassed and never stopped his delivery, as he watched his face in the mirror, being a tough guy. After an hour of adjusting his hair and delivering tough guy lines, he must have recognized that in addition to having his mother's kind eyes, he also had her thin eyebrows. So it was only natural to pencil them in to look thicker and appear more menacing and manly. When he was done using Mom's eyebrow pencil he looked more like Groucho Marx than Karl Marx.

Dad was now satisfied with what he saw in the mirror, so he went into the kitchen to make breakfast. I heard him go to the refrigerator; I heard him crack some eggs, but I didn't hear the scrambling of the eggs, I didn't hear the frying pan come out, or smell the butter frying in the pan. I was getting anxious to think I might be getting some eggs and breakfast that we could share, Dad and me. Instead of scrambled eggs for breakfast, Dad came out with the eggs in a bowl with the yolks missing. I watched him as he sat on the couch while I watched cartoons. He put his hands into the bowl and put the slimy raw eggs all over his face. I never saw anything like this before; I never heard of such a thing. I'm just a kid, so I think, *Maybe all fathers do this*, but in the back of my mind I knew this wasn't so. How could this be what fathers do? It just didn't look right.

With one eye on the TV and one eye on Dad, I watched as he applied this slimy mask over his face. I didn't say anything, I couldn't say anything, and I didn't know where to begin. When the eggs were all gone from the bowl and on his face, he put his head back and said, "I have to wait for this to dry and get hard, so I can't talk or it'll crack and it won't work, so don't talk to me." I sat on the couch with Dad and watched TV, quietly, as he sat motionless like a mummy, cautious not to move a muscle. He was afraid to move and crack his egged face. It was almost noon and I was getting hungry, so I got up off the couch, shut off the TV, and got dressed while Mom snored in the bedroom that we shared. I went downstairs to Harry's candy store and luncheonette. Since the eggs didn't become breakfast, I wanted lunch.

I passed Johnnie Moon, who stood guard at the door; I nodded, and said his name as I walked into Harry's. I sat at the counter and I saw Harry standing in front of the grill. Even though he knew my name, since he saw me all the time, he asked me, "What do you want, kid?"

"My usual," I said. "Burger, fries, and a cherry Coke."

As the fries were popping in the hot oil basket, and the burger was on the grill, Harry said, "Tell your father I want to see him; he owes me money, before he goes to the track." Harry meant racetrack, and before he lost all his money and couldn't pay what he owed Harry, for loans during the week and my food bills, because this was the only place I ate.

I looked at Harry and said, "I can't do it right now; he's got egg on his face."

Harry looked at me for a moment; his eyebrows went up, and then he let out a huge open-mouthed laugh. That was the first and only time I ever saw Harry laugh. As he laughed, he tried to speak. He couldn't get the words out — all he kept saying was, "Egg on his face, egg on his face, ha, ha, egg on his face," over and over again. He could hardly catch his breath. What did I say that was so funny? I just told Harry the truth. He had egg on his face!!! I'm just a kid, what do I know?

I asked one of the older boys, "What does it mean to have egg on your face?"

He said, "It means you're embarrassed, or you got caught with something you are ashamed of."

After I ate the burger and fries and drank the Coke, I went back upstairs to see my father. I asked him, "Dad, what are you ashamed of?"

He looked at me with his tight shiny face, barely moving his lips, like a ventriloquist, and said, "I have no idea what you're talking about. I'm not ashamed of nothing."

"Then why is there egg on your face?" I asked.

"You don't know what you're talking about — the egg on my face is because I'm Italian, and I had oily skin as a kid, and it left me with big pores. I put the egg on my face to shrink my pores, and make my face look tight."

I nodded my head up and down like I understood what he meant, but I really didn't. After Dad explained it to me, I thought maybe I should go back downstairs and tell Harry the real reason that he had egg on his face, but I thought, *What if I say something else that makes Harry laugh even more? So I'll just leave this one alone.* What do I know? I'm just a kid, and <u>so what</u> if he has egg on his face.

Hello, Ronald

ON WEEKENDS, AFTER school, when I wasn't over at Nanny's house, I went to see Grandma Pearl, Grandpa Meyer, and Stewie. This was my mother's side of the family. They lived on the 14th floor in The Bronx River projects. I went in the elevator and pushed the 14 button; it seemed like forever to get to the top floor if the elevator made a lot of stops. Grandma Pearl never locked the door, so anyone could walk in without her getting up to answer the door to let people in. Once inside, to the left was a living room. Grandpa Meyer was always on the plastic-covered couch watching a baseball game with his shoes and socks off, lying down on his back with his head propped up by a pillow so he could watch TV. Grandpa Meyer never attempted to get up or move to make room for you; his body language indicated he didn't want you there, and he didn't want you to share his couch. He wore stained striped boxer shorts and a dirty yellow strap T-shirt. I didn't think he could be my real grandfather; my other grandfather looked like a movie star — silk smoking jacket, ascot around his neck, black leather slippers.

When I walked in, Grandpa Meyer said, "Hello, Ronald." He never said another word to me until Sunday night when I went home. Then he would say, "Goodbye, Ronald." All day Saturday and all day Sunday, he just stayed on the couch watching baseball games, shoes and socks off, dirty stained boxer shorts, and the same stained yellow strap T-shirt. He never even got up to eat; Grandma Pearl would bring in food for him. He never thanked her or talked to her, either.

My other grandfather made such a fuss over me, watched TV with me, took me to the park on Saturday and church on Sunday. Those two men were so different — how could they both be my grandfathers? At seven I thought Grandpa Meyer didn't like me; in reality, he didn't like himself. He didn't take care of himself; he didn't care how he looked, or how he dressed. He didn't think enough of himself to have me get to know him. He never spoke to anyone, so I understood why he didn't speak to me. This man was so different from my "real grandfather." I thought he loved me less, but maybe he loved me the same. Grandpa Meyer kept his thoughts and feelings to himself, and being a kid, I never questioned it. He was a quiet man who led a quiet life; he touched no one while he was alive, and no one really knew him. He revealed nothing of himself and gave nothing back to anyone.

He died young. He was about sixty years old. At his funeral, there were no tears, no speeches, no stories … there was nothing. Just him in a box. We went back to the apartment and it didn't feel empty without him. Even at my young age, I knew this was no way to be. Grandpa Meyer taught me something: he taught me what NOT to be. Don't be so quiet that no one knows you — extend yourself to others. I thank Grandpa Meyer for showing me that communication skills are how we are measured. Our ability to interact and show our emotions is how we are accepted, judged, and loved. I know now that when I die, I want to be so well-known by my family and friends that there WILL be stories to tell about me and who I was. I'm just a kid, so I have a lot of time to make sure I don't turn into Grandpa Meyer.

Grandma Pearl

MY MOTHER'S MOTHER, my other grandma, is Pearl. Pearl, what a strange name — most names don't mean anything, but hers had meaning. A pearl comes from a shell in the ocean and is a rare prize worn in jewelry and traded like money all over the world by people. A pearl sounds like a good thing to be, since most names have no meaning, but hers did. In real life, Grandma Pearl wasn't much different, except for the oyster shell and the ocean part and the traded part. She was prized and appreciated by all those who knew her.

Grandma Pearl held daily penny card games so friends and neighbors would come to be fed, have the company of others and a few laughs, and win or lose a few pennies. Her kitchen table was always full of penny card players, men and women, young or old, of all races and religions. Some people spoke English. Some didn't. Grandma Pearl was a great diplomat; she was the United Nations of the penny card games. She and her friends played cards from the afternoon till midnight. Most of them had nowhere else to go and no family to go home to, so they were all alone together, which meant they would no longer be alone. They had each other. That penny card game represented food, friendship, laughter, and an occasional two-dollar winner's pot. On the countertop near the refrigerator there were all kinds of food. Everyone brought something from their own kitchen: a huge variety of Spanish food, Middle Eastern food, and some soul food. The men who couldn't cook brought cakes and cookies and soda from the supermarket. It was truly a grand buffet. Since

Grandma Pearl wasn't a good cook, she liked it this way; it all just worked out perfectly. It wasn't the money, the winning or losing that kept them together … it was that everyone had a place to go and a friendly opponent to sit next to — THAT'S what kept them together.

As I looked around the table at Grandma Pearl's card game, it taught me that it's not what you do that matters, it's who you're doing it with, and the game isn't so important. Just by sitting there, they were all winners. By watching the endless card games that went on every day, I learned social skills and social acceptance of others. That's what I took home with me when I left Grandma Pearl's house — that, and the Jamaican jerk chicken with rice.

Jimmy Moy

LIKE ALL CITY apartment buildings, the front and sides of the build-ings were storefronts. One of the storefronts in the front of 437 Morris Park Avenue had a sign on the window: "Chinese Laundry." I knew what Chinese food was, but I didn't know what Chinese laundry was. As we played in front of the store, I never saw Chinese people go-ing in or out of the store to do their laundry. I thought only Chinese people did their laundry there. I saw many people going in with pil-lowcases full of clothes, and some came in empty-handed and left with a square bundle of brown paper tied together with a string. I watched a while, and I figured out that the clothing in the pillow-cases became the neatly packaged brown paper bundles that people walked out with. One day while playing in front of the Chinese laun-dry, I decided to go inside and see for myself what went on. I opened the glass door that had Jimmy Moy printed in gold letters on it, and above my head, the door hit a big bell as it opened; with the sound of the bell, a small Chinese man with a white apron came out to see who had opened the door. Like walking into a bakery, it too had a smell, but not a good one. It smelled like chemicals. In the store it was very warm, and all the windows were fogged up from the heat.

The small man yelled, "What you want, boy?" I didn't know what to say, because I didn't want anything. The small man lifted up his arms and waved at the door. "Jimmy Moy say get out, boy — go home." I turned and ran for the door, hoping he wouldn't chase me, and come from behind the counter. This was not my only contact with Jimmy Moy, but it was the only thing he ever said. Every day he swept in front of the store, he would see us kids, and waving his hands like he was swatting at flies, he would yell, "Jimmy Moy say get out, boy, go away, go home." What Jimmy Moy didn't understand was that this was our home, the sidewalks in front of our building. This was where we played. Jimmy Moy never spoke to us or smiled, and we never got up early enough to see his store not open. We were never up late enough to see his store closed. Jimmy Moy ate and slept in his store, and no one knew anything about him except that he wanted you to go home.

Every year my mother got a calendar made of rolled-up bamboo with colorful pictures of dragons on both sides, and printed in the middle in big gold block letters was Jimmy Moy, just like his window. This calendar hung in the kitchen and hid the crack in the wall near the sink. Thanks to Jimmy Moy, I always knew what day it was, what month it was, and who gave it to us, since his name was on it ... Jimmy Moy. He was one of those people who were there every day of your life, but you never really saw them. He blended into the fabric of the neighborhood; he was just another hard-working local merchant in front of our building in The Bronx, trying to make a living from the tenants upstairs.

Bernie

THE STORE NEXT to Jimmy Moy's in the front of my building was Bernie's. Bernie's store was like a small supermarket; it had everything. You could get light bulbs, bread, milk, cold cuts, mops, brooms, detergent, Hostess cupcakes.... Everything! The store was very cramped, with every inch of space utilized. Behind the waist-high counter was Bernie, wearing a soiled white apron. Anything you could ask for, he knew where it was. If he couldn't reach it, by his side was a ten-foot pole that when you squeezed the bottom the mechanical fingers on the top would close and pull down any item off the upper shelves. Bernie was like an outfielder — when you asked for something, he would glance up, squeeze the bottom of the pole, and easily catch any item in his other hand before it fell on the ground.

Bernie was a big burly man, slightly overweight, but more big than fat. He was balding and never clean-shaven, and his hands were the size of a catcher's mitt — maybe that's how he caught everything. Bernie and his family lived in the building, and his store was always open. I never saw him when he wasn't working, even though we lived in the same building. Bernie had a wife and two sons. His wife was in a wheelchair. She was in her thirties, with pale white skin and red hair that was always neatly combed and pushed to one side. Her complexion reminded me of the cameo pin that Nanny wore on her scarf when she got dressed up. When the weather wasn't too cold, and all summer long, she would sit in her wheelchair outside the store. My eyes were always drawn to her legs, which she tried to keep covered with a small blanket. When I did see them, they were pale and smooth and thin, without a shape of muscle. She told me she had polio, and that's why she was in a wheelchair. I never knew her name, but she always smiled with a shy, beautiful smile when she saw you looking at her. The wheelchair took away her ability to walk, but not her smile.

Outside, next to her was her son, Peter. Peter also had what she called polio. He too had red hair and was in a wheelchair. Peter had shocking blue eyes that followed you slowly when you spoke to him. His voice was weak, and no matter how you tried to talk to him or play with him, he never responded. The wheelchair removed his smile, and having no smile removed his childhood. Peter had a brother. He was tall and thin, with an athletic build and curly black hair. He didn't resemble anyone in his family. He always played ball in the streets with the teenagers his age when he wasn't upstairs studying schoolwork. He was a quiet kid, and I hardly ever saw him.

Bernie knew me. I was always in his store because I was always hungry and Mom never shopped. Almost always when you were inside Bernie's store, there were a few people ahead of you. Bernie was always rushing; he worked feverishly fast to fill up your grocery bags, so you would leave, and he could help the next person. Even though I saw Bernie many times during the day, he never called me by my name. He just looked at me and said, "What do you want, kid?" He was always pleasant enough, but he didn't have time to talk to you because someone was always behind you waiting to buy groceries. My mom and dad had what you call a "tab" with Bernie. When I played outside and came into Bernie's store I could get anything I wanted, as long as I said, "Put it on my tab" after I took it. I learned this "tab" was in place of money. All during the week, no one probably had money, because most of the customers that were in front of me, after Bernie put their groceries in bags, they all said, "Bernie, put it on my tab; see you Friday." I learned later on that on Fridays, after work, my dad would pay the tab before he went upstairs to the apartment, just like everybody else. That's when I found out that on Friday, most people in my neighborhood got paid money from their jobs. Since Bernie ran tabs on most of the people in the neighborhood, that meant cash wasn't around until Friday.

Bernie was a well-liked and trusting neighborhood store owner, and what he realized was that we were all poor together, but we didn't know it because we all lived in the building above, and in the same neighborhood. This was our way of life. Everyone lived week to week, paycheck to paycheck, and thanks to Bernie, we didn't need cash to survive. As long as Bernie knew you, you could run a tab with him at his grocery store; you could eat today, and pay on Friday. He kept a composition notebook on the side of his cash register, and everyone had a page where he kept our tabs. You rarely heard the ring of the cash register drawer open; instead, you could see Bernie and his small black pencil writing in your tab.

Bernie was a well-respected man in our neighborhood; unfortunately, since he worked all the time he never got a chance to do anything but work, and keep our neighborhood going. I always wished that on Sundays, Bernie would close the store and put his family in a big station wagon, and drive off for the day, to a park somewhere, just like Mister Ducker on *Petticoat Junction,* but this was not TV; this was the life of Bernie, a man who owned a grocery store in The Bronx.

Catman

EVERY DAY AFTER the school bus dropped us off at three o'clock, some kids went home for milk and cookies, or to do homework and drop off their books and lunch boxes. The kids like me who weren't met at the bus went to Harry's candy store. After a chocolate egg cream and a doughnut, I went outside to play box ball or hit the penny. The pink rubber high-bounce ball for twenty-five cents was a Spaldeen. I learned later on as I got older it was a Spalding. Everyone in The Bronx called it a Spaldeen. Box ball was a shortened version of handball; we hit the ball back and forth from one concrete box to the other opponent's concrete box. When we tired of box ball, we put a penny in the crack of the cement walk and we paced back five steps and we each tried to hit the penny while the opponent opposite you did the same. This went on for hours, or until the older kids — usually the brothers of my friends — saw "him," and screamed at him: he was CATMAN. When you heard CATMAN all the kids my age, and the older kids all started yelling, tauntingly, CATMAN, CATMAN, CATMAN. Then someone would throw an empty soda can at him.

You see, every day at about five-fifteen, this pack of unruly and disrespectful children would band together like in *Lord of the Flies* and taunt him. He was a very large, poorly dressed, unshaven, balding man. He had high-top black work boots that made him lumber with each slow step he took. No matter what the season, he was always overdressed; in the summer his face was drenched in sweat that dripped onto his collar. He wore old farmer's blue jeans, torn at the knee and strapped over his shoulders, with a checkered long-sleeved shirt and a black heavy coat that stopped by his knees. In each of his hands were worn paper shopping bags. He walked with his head down past the children as they shouted CATMAN, CATMAN, and tossed cans at him. He made a right-hand turn at Harry's candy store and walked down Lebanon Street toward the lots under the train trestle.

At times the kids would hit him or come close, as they threw the cans; he would stop walking, but not turn around. The chanting of CATMAN never stopped, and by now eight or ten kids were following him. He slowly crossed the street and entered the lots with his young taunters behind him in pursuit. Before his descent into the lots, he turned and faked a charge like a bull in an arena; he took only a few steps, and the young pack of challengers ran with fear. CATMAN's large imposing body, unshaven face, and toothless snarl were intimidating. The kids ran as he turned, and he continued unescorted into the lots. We all ran back to the candy store and continued to be children instead of a wolf pack.

This went on almost every day, and finally my inquisitive nature decided to investigate further. I waited the next day up on Tremont Avenue near the train station for CATMAN. His five o'clock train must have brought him to Tremont Avenue every day after work. I saw him walk out of the train station, and down Tremont Avenue toward the candy store, I saw the little predators begin to gather, and decided not to join in. As he walked, I hid between the parked cars and the pack of taunting kids who threw cans at CATMAN, while shouting obscenities at him. I kept a safe distance out of anyone's sight, going from parked car to parked car, lying low at their bumpers. He walked the same way he always did, down past the candy store, down toward Lebanon Street with the kids in pursuit, and before he entered the lots, he turned, snarled, and gestured; his shoulders moved forward as if he were going to charge. Once again the bluff deterred his attackers and they retreated, running back to the candy store. I was now between two parked cars behind CATMAN. I didn't accept or run from his gestured charge.

He turned and went into the lots; my heart was racing, as I was trying not to be seen. I followed CATMAN. He walked slowly to a cement slab that held the iron foundation of the train tracks in place. He sat slowly and took off his heavy coat and put the two shopping bags alongside him. He reached his big hand into one of the bags and took out two big bowls. He laid one on his right side and one on his left side. He reached into the other shopping bag on his right side and pulled out three cans. From his overalls, he took out a can opener, and began opening the cans, one by one, and placed his hand back into the bag for a fork. He scooped out the contents of the cans into the bowl. He then reached into the other bag and took out a bottle of water and poured the water into the other bowl that lay beside him.

By now, fifteen to twenty cats of all sizes and colors surrounded him. His hands gently stroked the ones that rubbed against him; the little ones climbed all over his big body. Some were on his shoulders, some on his back; one little black cat was on his head as he opened his mouth and smiled. His smile didn't look menacing now, and his big body wasn't threatening. He laughed and touched the cats lovingly, stroking and feeding these forgotten alley cats. I watched his head turn to greet them all, and his eyes looked at each one, as if he knew to pet and stroke them all, not to leave anyone out. The big cats sat on his lap, the kittens clawed and tugged at him, all over his big body. I watched CATMAN and his cats for about an hour, hiding behind the iron train trestle. When the food and water were gone, and all his cats were touched and talked to, he packed away the empty cans and water bottle. He stood up, put on his coat, and leaned over to brush his cheek against the little calico kitten that sat near the water bowl. He said his goodbyes, lifted the shopping bags, and then he turned to walk.

I followed him out of the lots and down Tremont Avenue. He walked slowly, like each step was difficult for him; it was easy to stay hidden and follow him undetected, since his movements were so slow. I followed him to Tremont Avenue and West Farms, and then he went into a small old two-story building, where people rented rooms by the week. He walked up the steps through a glass door and when I could no longer see him, I ran back to my block, back to Harry's candy store. I never told the other kids where I was or what I saw.

The next day, about five-fifteen, the train brought CATMAN back to us, like every other day. But it wasn't like every other day to me. I felt different. I could not shout, taunt, or throw cans at CATMAN, like the others. I didn't see him as the big ugly misfit like the other kids did. They didn't see him like I saw him. Yesterday changed all that. I saw a big, gentle man with a big heart who cared for the stray alley cats that no one else cared about. I thought of him carrying the food and water on the train in those worn-out paper shopping bags, and how people looked at his ragged clothing and toothless smile and thought they knew him. They didn't know CATMAN like I did; those cats were his joy, in a life that showed him no companionship or respect. I couldn't take part in the children's taunting of CATMAN anymore.

So every day at five o'clock I left before he came off the train, before he walked down the block past Harry's, and the kids followed him, and threw cans, and mocked him as he walked into the lots to feed his cats. Instead, I went upstairs to watch cartoons and listen to my mother snore in the next room. I'm just a kid, but I know a good person when I see one, no matter what they look like or how other people see them. CATMAN taught me to see beyond the obvious, and judge for myself who a person truly is — by the way he treats others, and the stray cats in our neighborhood.

Sundays

IN THE WINTER months Granddad's room was very cold, so when I slept over, I slept in the living room. The steam radiator that hissed all night in the corner made the living room toasty warm. I slept on a fold-out aluminum cot with a one-inch mattress, with springs that creaked with every breath and movement I made. The mattress was so thin that I could count the springs that stabbed me all over my body. I was lucky I made it through the night without breaking a rib. Today, at 6:15 a.m., I wake up, wide awake, as only an eight-year-old can be. I opened the wooden cabinet door that hid the nineteen-inch black-and-white television. There was a lot to choose from, channel two through eleven, but on channel nine, I watched *Modern Farmer.* It's all about life on the farm: milking the cows; feeding the chickens, the pigs, and the goats; and turning out the horses. If you still had any energy left, you could drive the tractor and cut the wheat and make hay bales. I watched the entire program without blinking, careful not to miss a thing, as if there were going to be a test on everything I saw, even though I was in apartment seven, a third-floor walkup, on Crosby Avenue in The Bronx. Hey, you never know when this will come in handy.

After *Modern Farmer,* Heckle and Jekyll cartoons were on. Bugs Bunny and Wonderama with Sonny Fox would be on all morning. Nanny and I had toast for breakfast as she sat in the kitchen with her small round mirror in front of her, putting on her eyebrows. Nanny could put on her eyebrows faster than Zorro could slash a big Z on a fat man's butt. When we heard Granddad leave the bedroom, I ran into the living room, because the TV is on, and he'd say something like: "Nobody's watching TV, shut it off." But if I was sitting in front of the television, he just waved good morning to me.

Today is Sunday — a lot of things to do on Sunday. Grandad and I were going to church today; we were going to make the ten o'clock mass at Saint Theresa's Church up the Avenue. Today I was in my Easter suit, the one that Nanny buys me every year. I get to wear the suit on Easter and on spring break the following week to the Ringling Brothers Circus at Madison Square Garden, and on Sundays to church, and Christmas Day. She always bought the suit a little big, she said, so I "could grow into it, and have it last all year." She was right. Every year the suit started off like it was my big brother's, even though I didn't have one. By Christmas, the cuffs on the pants didn't scrape the ground anymore, and I could see my whole hand beyond the coat sleeves. This magical shrinking suit came with a long-sleeved white button-down collared shirt, with a ready-made snap-on green tie. I had to wear black socks instead of white sweat socks. On my feet were black loafers, with a gold and white buckle, that Nanny and I bought at Father and Sons Shoes on Westchester Square. What was so special about these shoes was that Granddad had the exact same shoes. Nanny always tried to dress us alike. Granddad and I never went shopping, so Nanny dressed us both.

We had to walk up Crosby Avenue past the train station to get to Saint Theresa's Church. During the walk, we held hands. He held my hand not so much because he loved me; he held it so I wouldn't run into the street. I always thought to myself, *How dumb does he think I am? Even though I'm just a kid, why would I want to run into the street and get hit by a car?* That didn't sound like a fun afternoon, and the thought of going to Jacoby Hospital in an ambulance sounded like even less fun. During the walk, we didn't speak as we passed the stores on the Avenue, but I could look in the windows — after all, we had to get to church on time. God is very punctual. He even starts church every hour, on the hour. Granddad was always serious on the walk to church, and I was instructed to follow him, and to do as he did, once inside.

Like a soldier following his sergeant, I entered the church doors, I reached into the white marble pedestal, hit the water that was in it, and with the same wet hand, touched my forehead, my stomach, my chest, my left side, then my right side. I had no idea what I was doing; I was just following Granddad. We walked through the doors with all the other people, and down the aisle; about halfway down, we stopped. Now Granddad knelt down on one knee and repeated the hand signals we just did a moment ago when we first entered the church. We all sat shoulder to shoulder, and a man called a priest prayed in a language I couldn't understand. I asked Granddad what he was speaking; he told me, "God's language." *So God speaks only in Latin?* I thought. *I don't know Latin, so God's not really talking to me, but I'll do what I'm told, and follow all the others.* I stood up when everybody stood up; I sat down when everybody sat down. We leaned forward and knelt on these red cushions in front of us when everybody else did.

Granddad gave me three pink envelopes, and told me when the bell rang and a straw basket was put in front of me, to put in one envelope. I had no idea what was going on, but I felt I had to keep quiet and follow Granddad and what everybody else was doing. I didn't understand why, if I had three envelopes, and they came around three times, and each time I have to put in an envelope, why couldn't I just put in all three envelopes at one time, and then the nice old man passing around the basket could sit down and rest the other two times? Every once in a while, I would look at Granddad while people were whispering. Later on he told me we were all praying. Praying — now that, I remembered. Nanny taught me a few prayers, but this didn't sound like anything I knew. I knew one thing —that Granddad's lips and everybody else's lips were not moving together. I knew he was just like me; he didn't know the prayers either. He was moving his lips, trying to fit in and be part of the good people, the church-going people. Then I remembered: Granddad was an actor. I had seen the photos in his room where he was different characters, and so, he was acting like he was praying. He was playing the part of a church guy. If he could be a cowboy, an Army general, and a musician, I guess he could be a church guy. I'm not sure if he knew what it meant to be a good Catholic, but he enjoyed dressing up, having an audience, and telling people, "I go to church on Sundays."

When church was over, on the walk back home, we stopped at the bakery to buy buns. Buns are the ancestors of doughnuts, since nobody called them doughnuts, even though they were the same thing. Granddad bought six buns: two jelly, two cream, and two crullers. They were placed in a white box and tied up with red and white string that hung from a spool on the ceiling. We walked back down Crosby Avenue to the apartment, and then went upstairs. Nanny was already dressed and cooking. Sometimes she would be on the phone talking to her sister Marion. She sat at a white desk in the hallway of the apartment. I could always tell when it was her sister Marion on the phone, because Nanny would be either whispering or laughing — sometimes laughing so hard she couldn't catch her breath. The more she laughed, the more Granddad looked displeased. He always thought something was going on behind his back, and they were talking about him.

When she got off the phone, she asked me how church was. I didn't know what to say, so I said, "Fine." People like fine. Fine is the answer to every question that hopefully doesn't start another question. I really didn't know how to feel about church. I didn't feel like I visited God or God's house. To me, it was a walk down Crosby Avenue; then I had to sit quietly, listen to words I didn't understand, speak in a low voice and follow what the others did, get doughnuts called buns, and come home. That was good enough.

I asked Nanny, "Why don't you go to church with us?" I saw women her age there.

She said to me, "They're all holy rollers — when I want to talk to God, I just do. You don't have to be in a church to talk to God." Next Sunday, if I didn't want to go to church, I'd remember what Nanny said, and see if it worked for me ... but deep down I knew I wouldn't; that would disappoint Granddad.

In the apartment, you could smell the aroma of Italian food cooking. Soon my aunt Ann and my cousin Wayne would be over for the two o'clock Sunday dinner that Nanny cooked. I loved seeing my aunt Ann. She was so pretty, and it was fun to watch her always looking in the mirror, and complimenting herself on how good she looked. With Aunt Ann came her son, my cousin Wayne. Wayne was seven years older than me, and the first grandchild in our family. Wayne is the alpha boy. He's much bigger than me, and he's a sneaky bully. When we were with the grown-ups, he was quiet and polite. When we were alone, I got punched, and choked, and wrestled to the ground. He practiced the latest wrestling techniques on me that he had seen on television during the week.

He was on a mission. His mission was to make me cry, and mine was to hold back the tears, or he'd call me a baby. He introduced me to the Nelsons. I met the half Nelson and the full Nelson, but not Ozzie and Harriet Nelson. Then came the sleeper hold. If he had been a little stronger, I would have been sleeping for a long, long time. We didn't play much together; I just got beaten up in all four rooms without anybody knowing it. It's a good thing Nanny lived in an apartment. If she'd lived in a house, it would have probably had a basement. Wayne would be in a white lab coat and I would be strapped to a table while he was doing medical experiments on me as Nanny cooked. Since Wayne loved Frankenstein, I could see myself coming up for dinner with lobster hands and a donkey's tail.

The living room turned into a dining room when the hall table was extended with wood inserts, then placed in front of the mirror in the living room. The family would eat for hours as Nanny served everyone, walking back and forth from the kitchen to the table, bringing out a small banquet. Wayne and I were allowed to go downstairs by ourselves after we ate dinner, since we couldn't sit there all those hours. He got a dollar, since he was older, and I got fifty cents. Then we walked two blocks to Garber's candy store. Our goal was to bring back as much as we could with a dollar fifty.

The owner of the candy store was an older man. He was only a few inches taller than me, and he spoke with an accent. He was missing his right thumb, and my eyes were always drawn to it, or the lack of it. He had numbers tattooed on his forearm. He also had a goal. Get you in to the candy store, take your money, and get out. He never smiled, and he had no patience. He stood behind the counter and yelled, "What do you want? If you don't know, get out!" There was no such thing as walking around or just looking. I had to be prepared before I entered the candy store, knowing what I wanted. Most weeks I went back to Nanny's apartment with candy or ice cream. This week it was a small lock with no key — that's why it was on sale. Nanny called him Garber the Robber. In his store nothing was perfect, and he always took advantage of the kids in the neighborhood. After dinner we watched *Wild Kingdom* with Marlin Perkins, and then *The Wonderful World of Disney*. By then, it was eight o'clock. Tomorrow would be Monday; everybody had to go back to work and school.

Nanny packed me what she called a "care package." In it were today's dinner leftovers. Her leftovers were better than most people's first time arounds. By the weight of the bag, I probably had enough food until Wednesday. When I got back to the apartment, I'd hide it in the refrigerator. It would be safe there. Since Mom didn't cook or shop, the refrigerator door never opened. I could hide a million dollars in the refrigerator, and a week later it would still be there.

Granddad drove me back to the apartment in the old black-and-white Chevy Biscayne. The weekend was over. I was clean, and had a swollen belly from eating so much. I survived Cousin Wayne's numerous attacks without crying or being called a baby. I even had a lock with no key, so I could use it only one time. The choke marks on my neck would probably disappear by morning when I was ready to go back to school at Public School 105. AAAHHH!!! What a weekend ... I couldn't wait to do it all again next week!

The Hanukkah Bush

GRANDMA PEARL KNEW the heart and spirit of everything. She knew how to share and enjoy all holidays. When it was the Fourth of July, when most parents told their kids, "No fireworks," she wanted them. She told me the loud noise of the fireworks was like the guns and cannons that went off during the battles that gave us our great country. When it was Halloween, she helped me and her son (my uncle) Stewie paint our faces, like ghouls dug up from the grave. She gave us bags of candy to get us started before we went door to door for trick-or-treat. Every occasion to celebrate, she did. When you're poor, like she was, the little things make you rejoice and capture festive moments.

Grandma Pearl had an assortment of health issues. She had diabetes, and heart problems. She was overweight and she couldn't walk well, so she didn't go out much. She never went anywhere. No vacations, no friends to visit. Her entire life centered on her friends in her building, and the card games she hosted. Her vision was poor, so she wore thick glasses all the time that hid her eyes. When her glasses did come off, she had blue eyes. She said she didn't have blue eyes, she said she had wall eyes, because one eye always looked at the wall — it didn't move back and forth like the other. She wasn't bitter about her eyes; she just wanted you to share a laugh with her when her glasses came off.

Grandma Pearl was the queen of the penny card games, and her door was always open and full of card players from The Bronx River project where she lived. She had friends of all nationalities and religions. When it was a religious holiday, she embraced that too. Grandma Pearl was Jewish, but as she put it, "a non-practicing Jew." I thought that meant either she was a perfect Jew, because she didn't have to practice, or she wasn't really Jewish. She told me that all religions are made up of good people, any person that believes in something spiritual is good. It doesn't matter if it's Catholic or Jewish or any other religion.

On her 14th floor where she lived, there was a family that were Seventh-Day Adventists, and they were very close friends; they constantly tried to enlighten her about their religion. She told all her card-playing friends that she loved their beliefs, and whatever crosses and medals or religious articles they wanted to give her, she would proudly display. She didn't do that to make them feel at home or comfortable — she did it because she believed all people believe in their own God. She told me she believed in Jesus, Jehovah, the Messiah, the Bible, the Torah, and any word of God. She believed that many people have many gods, and no one God is better than the other. She said there are so many people in the world, how can one God watch over them all? You need a lot of gods.

In her kitchen above the card table, which also was her kitchen table, there was a clock. Next to the clock was a big cross — not just a cross, but a cross with Jesus. On the opposite side of the clock there was a "Jewish star," as she called it, and a mezuzah next to it. She also kept the Bible by her bed even though she couldn't read it because of her poor eyesight. She said she felt safe having God in her house. She told me any God, all gods, were protecting her.

When spring arrived, Grandma Pearl welcomed in Passover and Easter. As winter arrived, she set up a Menorah by her Christmas tree. Since I spent more time with my other grandmother, my Nanny, around any religious holiday she celebrated, she celebrated as a Catholic. Granddad went to church while she cooked Sunday dinners. They celebrated Easter, Ash Wednesday, Lent, Palm Sunday, and on Fridays they ate only fish sticks and baked macaroni — no meat. Everything that was on Saint Teresa's calendar that hung on the wall, they celebrated. My two sets of grandparents never spoke to each oth-er or visited each other. It wasn't because they didn't like each other; they didn't even know each other. They each disapproved of who their child had married. Nanny didn't like my mother, and Grandma Pearl didn't like my father. Who could blame them, since this match wasn't made in anyone's heaven.

Nanny knew Grandma Pearl was Jewish, so when I told her that Grandma Pearl had a Christmas tree, she said that was impossible. I tried to tell Nanny how Grandma Pearl lived her life in the projects and that she had friends of all religions, and how she believed in all religions. Again, Nanny said, "That's impossible." She said, "She shouldn't have a Christmas tree; they are Jewish." That weekend, like most weekends, I had to be dropped off somewhere, and this was my weekend to be with Grandma Pearl and Uncle Stewie. I was excited to play with Uncle Stewie — he was only two years older than me — but I was uncomfortable because I had to tell Grandma Pearl that she wasn't allowed to have a Christmas tree. When I got to her apartment on Friday night, to the left of the door where you entered was the liv-ing room, with the big Christmas tree all lit up. Now Grandma Pearl and I had to have a talk. I sat down in the kitchen next to her and tried not to look at her, because I was serious, and sometimes her wander-ing eye would distract me, so I avoided eye contact.

"Grandma," I said as I looked at the floor, "I found out you can't have a Christmas tree — you're Jewish, and Jews can't have Christmas trees."

"Who told you that?"

Even though I felt like a tattletale, I told her, "My nanny said so." Grandma Pearl started to laugh. She laughed so hard I could see she didn't have her false teeth in her mouth. Now, I didn't want to look at her mouth because she had no teeth, and that would distract me. She continued to laugh until she cried, so her glasses came off to wipe her eyes. Now I was trying not to look at Grandma Pearl with no teeth and her crazy eye because I knew I couldn't be serious, and I would start laughing.

I stood up and took her hand and said, "Come with me." I walked her into the living room and stood in front of the Christmas tree. I said, "See, you can't have that — you can't have a Christmas tree."

She stopped laughing and looked at me and said, "Go back and tell your grandmother it's a Hanukkah bush, not a Christmas tree."

I looked at her, and looked back at the Christmas tree, and said, "Your Hanukkah bush looks like Nanny's Christmas tree."

She smiled and said, "Tell your nanny to enjoy the holidays and don't worry about my Hanukkah Bush."

Since both my grandparents had Christmas trees, I realized that they were like each other around the holidays, except Nanny didn't have a Menorah.

Marie Kissed Me

MARIE LIVED IN my building on the fifth floor. She was three years older than me. She told me she was Italian — even though her parents were born here, her last name ended in a vowel (that's what her mother told her) and that's how she knew she was Italian. She had a dark olive complexion, and her eyes were big and warm and soft. I told her she had eyes like Bambi. Her doe eyes revealed her calm, gentle demeanor. Marie was a head taller than me; maybe that was the attraction. I was her cute little guy — she liked to mother me and cuddle me and hug me. She was very physical, always brushing up against me and rubbing my shoulders. I never minded the attention. She would hold me in her arms. I could always smell the Juicy Fruit gum in her mouth that she always chewed. She chewed with her mouth open and when she smiled, you could see she had a chipped front tooth that made her look younger than her age and very cute.

When we would play outside of the building, she usually played with the girls, but when she saw me looking at her, she would wink at me and put her lips together, and blow me a kiss. When the playing stopped, she put her arm over my shoulder and walked me to sit with her on the fender of a car that was parked in front of the building. I never pulled away or thought anything was wrong with this. Once there, we leaned against the car, and she took me in her arms and cuddled me, and I liked it. Most of the kids that saw us would stop and make kissing sounds, as if to make fun of us. We never thought it was wrong or embarrassing, so we continued to hold each other.

Marie would tell me they were just jealous, and not to mind them. Somehow I knew to enjoy her affection in public; even at my age, it made me feel so grown up.

This went on all summer, the hugging and the cuddling. Then "IT" happened, "IT" being our first kiss. It happened so fast — with her arm on my shoulder, she pushed my head toward hers and our lips met. It was only a second that our lips touched, and I felt a tingle of electricity that shocked through my body, like I just put my finger on an electric socket. Now, not only could I smell her Juicy Fruit gum, I tasted the sweetness from her lips. After the kiss, her big brown eyes fluttered rapidly like a butterfly's wings, and her chipped-tooth smile was broader than before the kiss. Marie was such a great kisser. Her soft pink lips were always moist, as she licked them constantly while she chewed her Juicy Fruit gum. All the kids on the block witnessed the kiss, and now we were officially boyfriend and girlfriend.

At nine years old, I didn't realize how serious that was. Since my only responsibility in being a boyfriend was to kiss and cuddle, I didn't mind. Marie and I broke the ice with that kiss. Now, every time we cuddled, we kissed, and that was all the time. All the kids in the neighborhood from that day on called me "Marie's little boyfriend." They said it to be cruel and tease me, but instead it made me feel special. I had something none of the other nine-year-old boys had…a girlfriend.

Even now, whenever I see a package of Juicy Fruit gum, or smell the sweet breath of someone chewing it, I think of Marie and her sweet kisses, and how my whole body tingled when she kissed me for that very first time.

Frank the Fruit Man

ON THE STREET level of the apartment building on Morris Park Avenue, in The Bronx where I lived, next to Bernie's grocery store, was Frank the fruit man. Old man Frank sold fruits and vegetables in the storefront and out on the sidewalk, on wooden crates and stands. Frank was an older man; he was short, and thin. He wore a black leather cap on his head, even in the summer when it was hot. Since he wore an apron down to his knees, we never saw what clothing he wore underneath, but he always looked bundled-up and overdressed. Inside his store, it smelled like grass after it rained. All over the store there were big hanging scales to weigh the fruits and vegetables. There was no chair in the store, since Frank never sat down. He was always cleaning and unpacking fruits and vegetables. His wooden display cases were lined up with care; they never looked out of place. All the fruits and vegetables were placed by hand, one by one, row by row, in a straight line. They looked like the cornfields that they came from. I never saw a farm, but this was what I imagined a farm stand looked like.

Frank was from Italy and he had a very strong Italian accent. Sometimes when he spoke, you couldn't understand him. You understood about one out of three words he said, but it was enough for him to communicate everything. Frank was a soft-spoken man; when he did speak, he never raised his voice. He used his hands a lot when he spoke, and if you watched his hands, somehow, you understood him better. His gestures were that good. When the women shopped there, if they asked Frank a question, he put his hand to his cheek and twisted it, and somehow, that meant "It is good."

"Frank, is the watermelon sweet?" The index finger turned clockwise in his cheek, meant "Yes, it's good." When something was very good, Frank opened his eyes really wide and shook his head from side to side. That meant it was even better than the finger twist in the cheek. Frank knew all the kids in the neighborhood, and in the summer he would cut up pieces of watermelon and sell it to us for five cents per slice. Once in a while one of the kids would steal from Frank, if he was in the store with customers and too occupied to stand guard over his fruits. I liked Frank, and I felt protective of Frank, and I wasn't going to stand there and do nothing while someone stole from Frank.

One afternoon my friend Paulie put a few peaches in his pocket and didn't pay Frank. I didn't want to betray Paulie, but my desire to look after Frank was stronger than being friends with Paulie, especially because it was wrong to steal. When I told Frank what Paulie did, he said, "Gooda boy, nobody likes a teef." He pointed his fingers in the air as he said it. He then rewarded me with a watermelon slice for my honesty. Honesty that day was the sweetest policy, especially on a hot summer's day when you don't have a nickel.

The Funzy Circus Comes to Town

EVERY FEW WEEKS the apartment door would fly open, and a tall thin man with bushy hair and a laugh like a hyena came to visit. As soon as he walked in the TV was turned off, and the volume in our quiet apartment was turned up. I was told to call him Uncle Funzy — whether we were related or not, I wasn't sure; it just felt right to call him uncle, and it made us closer to think of him as family. Uncle Funzy walked in with his arms full of paintings and canvas, brushes, and paints. He was an artist. Funzy lived upstate in Margaretville, New York. When he wasn't in The Bronx selling his paintings, he was upstate with his family. His wife's name was Deloris. They had two kids: a boy, Frankie; and the baby, Rosie — a chubby strawberry blonde with red rosy cheeks.

Funzy could paint anything and when he was done it looked so real, it looked more like a photograph than a painting. He painted street scenes of Paris, oceans, mountains, clowns, animals.... Anything. He prided himself not only on the quality of his artwork, but the speed with which he could manufacture it. Canvas after canvas, these speedy masterpieces flowed from his hands. He mixed the colors on a paint board, and kept three brushes in his mouth, which he switched back and forth to suit the width of his brushstroke. As he painted, he told my father to look through the paintings he brought with him that he painted while home in Margaretville. He told my father, "If you see anything you like, take it; I'll make another one in a few minutes." My father didn't like taking paintings from Funzy, since this is how he made a living; he wanted Funzy to go home with money instead of hanging a picture on the wall. His paintings and canvases filled our small apartment, and downstairs, parked in front of the building, was Funzy's van filled with paintings and art supplies. There were paintings, brushes, paint cans, and tubes of paint everywhere, piled up to the roof. The only bare space was the driver's seat, and even that was smeared with paint, like a rainbow.

As soon as he arrived, we could feel the excitement and chaos Funzy brought with him. The music from the hi-fi came on, and to celebrate their reunion, they passed around thin stinky cigarettes that they inhaled and coughed as they laughed and sang oldies as uncle Funzy painted. Dad called out, "Funzy, do a horse! Funzy, do a Roman scene! Funzy, do an ocean!" With speed and his amazing talent, Funzy pumped out canvas after canvas of quality artwork. Magic flew from his hands. He took a blank canvas, and a complete masterpiece was finished in five or ten minutes — he moved like a machine. How he created and completed his artwork was just incredible to witness. He used primitive old brushes, and empty paint cans, sticks, and metal knives to spread the paint around on the canvas.

He possessed a humble charm about his talent. After he finished a new painting, and we told him how great it was, his only reply was," **It's okay, I'm no Michelangelo."** He didn't see himself as the great artist he truly was. As he painted, he talked and laughed with my dad, without missing a stroke, even with the brushes in his mouth. When he laughed, his teeth were clamped down on the brushes, so he laughed through his teeth. This made him sound like a hyena from a Tarzan movie. He and dad smoked the thin stinky cigarettes, while the music played in the background. With Funzy there, he created a carnival-like atmosphere. We were all happy and entertained. His creativity and energy filled the room. For me, he painted clowns — some sad, some silly.

As Funzy painted, with me in the living room, Dad went into the refrigerator for leftovers for Funzy. I had brought home food from Nanny's house a few days ago; she called it a "care package." She never let me go back to the apartment empty-handed. We knew that with Funzy's level of energy, sometimes he forgot to eat. Every year around Easter, Nanny took me to the circus. As soon as we entered Madison Square Garden, you felt it: an overpowering feeling of excitement. There was music, there were lights, and there were animals, clowns, hot dogs, popcorn, soda and so many things going on all at one time. That's how I felt when Funzy came to the apartment. The apartment came to life like a circus when Funzy came to town. Music, food, laughter, and excitement filled the apartment. Uncle Funzy was the ringmaster — he made it all happen. He created the electricity that lit up our quiet, dark apartment. He made everything fun just being around him. I thought that was why we called him Funzy. Later on, I learned his name was Alfonse, and his close friends and family called him Funzy, for short.

Late into the night, Funzy would fall asleep on the couch, with tubes of paint surrounding him like a colorful blanket, and a paintbrush still in his mouth. I slept on the floor next to him. I was too excited to go to bed, and I didn't want to miss the show he put on, since he was the main attraction. In the morning when I woke up, he was always gone. The circus packed up and left our town. Once again it was dark and quiet in the apartment, until the next time The Funzy Circus came to town. I knew after he sold his paintings, in a few weeks, he would need more money, so he'd be back. He always came back. Uncle Funzy brought color to the otherwise blank canvas that was of our lives. Maybe I should wait at the door with some popcorn and a flashlight around my neck to welcome in the ringmaster and his circus, but for now, I *had to go to school.*

Johnny Mangino

JOHNNY MANGINO CAME from a neighborhood a few blocks from mine called The Five Corners in The Bronx. It was down Morris Park Avenue, about five minutes away. He was very short, only a few heads taller than me. He didn't work – or at least not work as we knew it. He was always at the bar next to Harry's, surrounded by other people's wives. My mother was one of these women. He was fast to buy drinks for everyone, even me. When he saw me, he would say, "There's Buster's kid — you want a soda?" Buster was my father's nickname. I knew that because he had a tattoo on the inside of his forearm with Buster written on it in faded blue ink. On his other arm was my mother's nickname, "Candy."

Johnny dressed like it was confirmation day at the church. He wore a black suit and white shirt with a black tie, and his black shoes were always shiny and polished. His pants were pressed with a sharp knife-like crease. His hair was black and combed straight back and flat against his head. His hair always looked wet. In his left hand there was a lit cigarette, and as he stood at the bar, a drink was in the other hand. He reminded me of the guy on my granddad's record covers, Dean Martin, only smaller. When Johnny talked, his shoulders would go up at the end of each sentence like a period. That's how you knew he was done speaking. Behind his back the people in the neighborhood called him "Little Johnny," but to his face it was "Johnny" or " The Mange" (short for Mangino). He always looked happy and when he smiled, which was after every sentence, and after every shoulder shrug; he smiled widely, with two big rabbit-like front teeth. His smile and gestures were so pronounced that whoever he was with laughed with him, almost on cue, after Johnny smiled.

Johnny was never without his very big best friend and strongman,"Pudgy." Pudgy was a mountain of a man; he was as tall as the doorway and just as wide. His bigness made Johnny look even smaller than he was, and standing next to Johnny made Pudgy's bigness even bigger. Both Johnny and Pudgy knew my mother and father. Those two and Funzy were the only friends they both shared. While at the bar, Johnny bought drinks for Mom, and when Dad came home from work, or some weekends, they would all get together. Once in a while, Johnny and Pudgy came up to the apartment. They would smoke those thin, stinky cigarettes with Dad, and they would all listen to records, and sing doo-wop.

When I saw Johnny in the street or outside the bar, he would call to me: "Come here, Buster's kid," and he would give me a dollar and tell me to go buy myself something, right after the smile and the shoulder shrug, and I always did.

My dad said Johnny was a great guy and always had a lot of money. He said Johnny was a loan shark. He was like a bank; he gave people money and they gave him back more money. Being a loan shark sounded like a good thing to be. He was always well-dressed, he had a crowd of people around him, and he was always happy.

One day when I was in front of Harry's candy store next to the bar, playing hit the penny, three police cars pulled up in front of the bar. Two policemen from each car jumped out of their cars and into the bar. There was a lot of shouting, and you could hear the bar chairs hitting the floor. Within seconds Johnny came out of the bar in a choke hold, as he was being dragged out onto the sidewalk. Johnny was struggling to break free; he looked like a helpless child in a headlock as the policeman held him. He looked so small and fragile in the arms of the bigger policeman.

As the two men wrestled, Johnny yelled for Pudgy. "He's choking me, he's choking me. Pudgy, come help me," he called over and over again. Pudgy burst from the bar and was making his way toward Johnny to help him get free from the policeman's choke hold. As he headed toward Johnny to free him, the other policemen saw Pudgy, and they jumped on Pudgy to stop him, and hold him back. Big Pudgy, with two policemen on him, struggled to get to Johnny. He easily threw off the policemen one by one, since their strength was no match for his. Pudgy reached Johnny, and the policeman who had him in a choke hold; he grabbed the policeman from behind and lifted him off the ground. Johnny broke free as big Pudgy wrestled with the policeman.

Johnny ran toward the street to get away, but another policeman grabbed him. Within a few seconds, Johnny was surrounded and pushed to the ground with three policemen on top of him. Pudgy had the policeman that held Johnny off the ground with his big arms wrapped around the policeman's neck. Pudgy wasn't letting go. The policeman struggled to get free, and now, two more policemen surrounded Pudgy in a fight to subdue him and free their partner from Pudgy's grip. As the two men punched him in the face, he turned to fight them both, letting go of the policeman he was choking. He lunged forward at the policemen with his outstretched arms as they both continued to punch him. He shook off the punches and put one in a headlock; he grabbed the other one by the throat and turned his body and put the other policeman in a headlock. Now Pudgy was holding on to both policemen. Each man was tucked under his huge arms with only their heads sticking out from under Pudgy's chest. Their hats were on the ground, and their uniforms opened up, as their buttons were ripped off in the scuffle.

As Pudgy held the two policemen in his massive arms, his eyes darted back and forth looking for Johnny as he yelled, "Run, Johnny — run!" He couldn't see that Johnny was on the ground already in handcuffs as the policeman held him on the sidewalk with his knee in Johnny's back. The other two policemen that were free ran over to the entangled men with their night sticks out. They raised their sticks and furiously hit Pudgy in the head, over and over. As they pummeled his head, blood flowed from Pudgy's scalp and ran down his face and into his eyes. His only concern was Johnny. He continued to yell, "Run, Johnny – run!" but now his voice was getting weaker as he screamed for his friend. As the men continued to pound him unmercifully on his head, the weary giant went down on one knee. He held on to the policemen as the other two continued to pound his head with their sticks. After a few more blows to his head, Pudgy hit the ground. The two policemen managed to wiggle free from his grip as his body went limp and unconscious. Blood was everywhere.

Pudgy lay on his back, his eyes half open briefly, and a faint whisper came from his bleeding mouth. "Johnny, Johnny, run … Johnny, I got 'em." As Johnny looked on in handcuffs, the big bear of a man lay there motionless, bleeding from his head and face. As Johnny looked on, tears were running down his face. There was a big crowd circled around us. All the people from the bar and candy store spilled out onto the sidewalk like ants around melting ice-cream, partly in curiosity, partly in horror, to see two neighborhood tough guys like Johnny and Pudgy in the hands of the police. Johnny was led away in handcuffs; the police kept pushing him toward the car. They shoved and kicked him into the back seat as they slammed the door behind him, his face pressed against the window to look for Pudgy. Pudgy lay there bleeding, motionless.

Two of the policemen pushed back the people that crowded around Pudgy, as the pool of blood spread out along the sidewalk. The other two policemen stood over his still body, aggressively holding their sticks as if the giant was just sleeping, waiting to awake and continue the battle. To judge from the blood on the sidewalk, Pudgy had lost the battle. His skull was no match for the pummeling of the night sticks the policemen gave him. It felt like forever, but soon the ambulance did come. It took four men to lift Pudgy onto the stretcher and carry him to the ambulance. His eyes never opened, and he never moved as the men tugged and lifted his giant body. As the ambulance pulled away, the crowd of onlookers — some friends, some just curious — left the sidewalk, and went back to doing what they were doing before the police and ambulance arrived twenty minutes earlier.

I knew both of these men. And even though there were small-time neighborhood criminals, in my mind the police were the criminals that day. I'm only seven, and it's hard to make sense of what just happened. Johnny and Big Pudgy were our friends … they were part of our neighborhood. They didn't seem like bad guys; they were more like celebrities. They laughed and bought drinks for everyone. Somehow, you didn't fear them; you felt safe around them, and if you needed money, Johnny pulled out a wad of cash and said, "See you Friday," after he shrugged his shoulders and smiled, and took a sip of his drink. I wondered what would become of that well-dressed happy little guy, and the gentle giant who followed him everywhere.

A week went by and I asked my father, "How's Johnny and Pudgy?" since I hadn't seen them around the neighborhood.

He said, "Pudgy never opened his eyes again, and he died in the hospital, and Johnny's okay; he paid for the funeral."

All my life I was told that policemen are good, to listen to them, and to obey them. In my mind, they weren't the good guys anymore.... Look what they did to Pudgy.

Big Alice

BIG ALICE WAS Harry's daughter. Harry owned the candy store and luncheonette on the corner of Morris Park Avenue and Lebanon Street in The Bronx. Harry's was the center of everything in our neighborhood. Alice was only twelve years old, but she had already filled out and had an hourglass figure. She was what you call big-boned. She was already about six feet tall and adolescently chunky. Even though she was a big girl, she possessed the charm of a little girl when she smiled. Her features were perfect. She had straight white teeth, a small thin upturned nose, and big brown eyes that hid behind long curved lashes. Her hair was long and shiny and held off her forehead by a headband that matched whatever color clothes she wore. Alice was blessed with all this, and she had her dad's candy store, which gave her instant popularity. Any new items that Harry sold in his store, she had one first. Anything she played with could create a new fad on the block just by her having it. She was that powerful. She had the first hula hoop, the first big pastel chalk to write in the street with, the first balsa wood airplanes, the first Wiffle ball and plastic bat. She introduced the neighborhood to jump ropes, baseball cards, paddle ball on a string, and every new toy that arrived at her dad's candy store. She had everything, and she knew it.

Alice beamed with confidence as she walked a head taller than anyone else. She was even taller than most kids' older brothers and sisters from the neighborhood. All this, and being Harry's daughter — how lucky can you get? You never wanted to get on her bad side; her father wouldn't let you into his store if you weren't okay with Alice. When it came to candy, Alice got to sample all the candy first. She would walk around with liquid-filled wax sticks, jawbreakers, fruit chewing gums, wax lips, and my favorite: the orange wax harmonica that actually played. In the summer she would tempt us all as she walked around with Italian ices and Dixie Cup ice cream.

Being an only child, instead of wanting a brother or sister, I wanted Alice, and only Alice, to be my sister. That would mean I, too, could share all the bounty Alice possessed, and since she was older and twice my size, I would never fight with her. I would be the perfect little brother. That meant Harry would be my father, and I could go behind the counter and make anything I wanted, from multi-flavored sodas to crazy ice cream combinations smothered in chocolate, vanilla, and strawberry syrup. I could grill burgers and hot dogs and serve them together on the same bun with a pile of pickles on top. Kids would come from other neighborhoods just to try my pickle dog burgers. What a life, what a dream come true. Being Alice's brother would also mean that I was untouchable. No one would want to mess with me and not be allowed entrance to Harry's kingdom of everything good and everything tasty. I would get picked first for every game that we played. I could treat all my friends to anything in the candy store. Since Harry's was the place to be, the place to go, I would be heir to the throne — "little Prince Ronnie." What a sweet spot to be in! Of course, this didn't happen.

So the next best thing was to be good friends with Alice. This wasn't hard, because she was easy to be with. She had so much going for her; she had nothing to prove. She was neighborhood royalty. Alice ruled when it came to sports, too. She was bigger and stronger than all of us. She could play punch ball and underhanded make two-sewers home runs when she hit the ball. By being tall like she was, those long legs could run faster than all of us. On the rare occasion that things didn't go her way, when she approached you and towered over you, and raised her voice, you immediately dropped to the ground and rolled over on your back like a puppy. Nobody wanted to fight Big Alice. Her size, and the thought of being banned from the candy store, were like a suit of armor for Alice. Even if you thought you were Superman, Harry's candy store was Kryptonite.

Alice was older than most of us, but younger than the kids who were my age who had older brothers and sisters. Being older was always a position of strength in my neighborhood. If she was in the older group of kids, she would be the youngest, since they were fifteen- and sixteen-year-olds. So Alice stayed with us and reigned supreme over the younger, smaller kids like me. Behind her back, because she was so big, the kids called her "Baby Huey," after the cartoon character who was clumsy and was taken advantage of because of his size. To her face, no one would dare call her that. Big Alice was approaching womanhood and she was developing faster than all the girls on the block. She already had breasts, and a big round shapely bottom. Her jeans fit her tighter than the other girls. The other girls looked like boys with long hair, next to her. They weren't curvy like Alice.

It's winter and it's cold outside. We still played outside on the block and in front of Harry's candy store. To break the wind, we leaned against the doorways of the building to keep warm as we talked and stayed outside. When I got cold, I would ask Alice to warm me up. She would open up her pea coat and cuddle with me for warmth. I wrapped my arms around her and she did the same. I could feel her soft breasts against me as we both hugged each other tightly. I would press up against her, and she swayed back and forth so we could hold each other and get our bodies even closer. If I held her any closer, I'd be behind her. We both giggled as we cuddled. We never spoke about our embraces and what was really happening. I enjoyed being pressed up against her breasts, and she enjoyed me pressing up against them as we hugged each other like Eskimos.

We both giggled, and she asked me, "What's so funny?"

I said, "Nothing." She also couldn't stop giggling, so I asked her the same thing: "What's so funny?"

She also said, "Nothing," but we both knew it WAS something. We were both being stimulated by each other without being brave enough to admit it. Being cold was an excuse for our cuddling fore-play. It was a long winter, and every chance I got, I told Alice how cold I was, and that she should keep me warm. She opened her coat and invited me in to cuddle — such innocent and natural behavior toward each other, but this was very exciting for both of us. We really didn't know why … or did we? We just couldn't talk about it.

This went on until winter was over. Since I enjoyed cuddling with Alice so much, I hoped winter would never end. I wanted New York to turn into Alaska! We were good close friends, so we were able to get away with it without admitting to one another what was really going on. It also worked well because of the difference in our ages. I was a cute little kid, and she was one of the big kids and "the leader of the pack." No one took our behavior seriously, since we could never be boyfriend and girlfriend, so somehow, it was okay. Winter unfortunately came to an end, and since Alice and I were so close, she asked me about Marie. Marie was another older girl on the block whose cute little boyfriend I had become last summer.

Alice said, "I know you make out with Marie; everybody on the block has seen you two." Even though Alice didn't like me "like that," she was hinting around that she wanted to use me to practice "mak-ing out," so she could get ready for the older boys.

This was a new level in our friendship. I guess after breast cud-dling all winter, it was only natural that "making out" was the next step in our friendship. We went into my building, and went under the staircase, and we practiced "making out." At first, we were un-comfortable, and giggled a lot, but Alice, being older, took control. I was so much shorter than her. The only way our mouths lined up was if I sat on her lap, so I did. Her lips were bigger than mine, and her mouth was so much bigger that when I puckered up, she put her lips over my whole mouth. It was more like getting your lips stuck into a milk bottle than a kiss. Her kisses were harder than Marie's — after all, she was bigger and stronger. This was just practice for Alice, and I was already broken in on how Marie kissed. We giggled and kissed, kissed and giggled, until she said she'd had enough. She made me promise not to tell anyone what we did, how we "made out." I promised. After all, Alice was my special friend and Harry's was my special place.

We left from under the staircase and went out of the building onto the street. We saw our friends playing outside and we joined them. I couldn't take my eyes off Alice, and every time she saw me looking at her, she smiled and winked at me. We had our secrets that we shared, and our moments of unspeakable closeness. Hey, I'm just a kid ... and Alice is almost a woman, and for a kid my age **... WOW!!!**

ASPCA

ON WEEKENDS, ALL the kids were off from school and out for the day, playing in front of the building. Since there were five of us, we were braver than usual. We waited on the corner of Tremont Avenue and Morris Park for the traffic to die down. It was a busy street with trucks and cars and buses speeding by. When it was safe to do so, we ran real fast across the street so we wouldn't get hit by the oncoming traffic. We saw a big brick and cement-block building with glass doors in front. Above the doors were the initials ASPCA Inside the building there were dogs barking behind chain-link and glass enclosures. It looked like a prison for animals.

The big dogs were kept with big dogs. The small dogs were kept with dogs their own size. There were cats and kittens of all sizes behind a similar holding cage, but the cats were quiet and poised. They sat motionless, looking forward like the Sphinx ceremonial cats. When you went near their holding pen, they remained stoic and quiet. They didn't charge up to the front, curiously, like the dogs did. The dogs were barking and running, playfully nipping at each other. They came to the front of the cages so they could be touched, and licked your hand through the metal gates. I sat cross-legged on the cold concrete floor in front of the metal gate, so I could pet the dogs. They were as curious about me as I was about them. Some sniffed and licked, as they wagged their tails; some barked. What I enjoyed most was watching them carelessly playing with each other; even though they were caged, their free spirits were evident as they ran in the confines of their cages.

One small long-haired brown and tan mixed breed stayed in the front of the chain-link gate opposite me. I stroked his head and he licked me a few times. When I got up to walk to the big dog pen, he also got up and joined his playful pack, and they resumed nipping and barking at each other. Men in gray uniforms walked around the building and went into the dogs' pens, to feed and give water to the dogs and cats, and to clean their cages. After we examined all the dogs and cats in their pens, we left the building and walked around back to the grassy hill behind the ASPCA. We explored the hill; we found bottles and rocks and sticks and relocated them all by throwing them into the bushes and broken trees. In the distance we heard the barking dogs from the shelter as we played. We all had a good time, and soon we went back across Tremont Avenue to the familiar front of our building to play.

A few days came and went, and once again we braved the crossing of Tremont Avenue to play with the dogs at the ASPCA. As soon as we passed through the big glass doors, we heard the loud barking of many dogs. We went to the big dog pen; there were fewer dogs than just days ago. I walked over to the small dog pen to look for the cute floppy-eared dog that had licked me. He was gone, and there weren't as many dogs in the pen as we had seen just a few days ago. There were new dogs mixed in with some I remembered. I sat in front of the cage and lots of dogs came to the gate for me to pet, and rubbed up against my hand. The one I liked, the one I came back to see, wasn't there. I didn't know what happened to him, or to the other dogs that were also gone. Maybe they all found homes with kids to play with who would take care of them. I thought to myself how wonderful that would be.

After walking around a while and looking in all the pens full of cats and dogs, we left the building. It was quiet when we left the building — no loud barking from the dogs who wanted to be noticed. We walked around back to play on the hill. As we ran, we threw sticks and tin cans at each other playfully, not really wanting to hit each other. We saw the men in the gray uniforms in the back of the building. This time the men had gloves on their hands that went up to their elbows. They wore masks on their faces covering their noses and eyes. They walked together, and each man opened one side of big gray doors that were locked in the middle. The men reached inside the doors and pulled out dogs one by one, and threw their quiet lifeless bodies into a green dumpster over their shoulders. When the dogs were big, one took the front legs, and the other took the rear legs and tossed these once-barking, running dogs into the dumpster, where they lay motionless, and stiff. Some had their eyes open, and their pink tongues were hanging out of their mouths to the side. I saw the little brown and tan dog that had licked me as I petted him. He looked like he was sleeping. But even at seven, I knew he was dead, even though I had never seen anything dead before. We were all silent. We knew we saw something we shouldn't have seen.

We all ran back across Tremont Avenue, this time not watching traffic as much. We were in a hurry to get back to Harry's candy store to tell the older boys what we saw. Harry was behind the soda counter and listened in as we talked. He leaned in toward us and said, "All those dogs are strays and they keep 'em for a week, and if nobody takes 'em, they gas 'em, to make room for the new dogs." Just like that, he told us how they killed those poor dogs, without any emotion in his voice, forgetting for the moment that we were just little kids. He didn't spare our feelings. He told us the harsh reality of it all.

I wished we had never seen what they did at the ASPCA. One day the men in the gray uniforms gave food and water to the dogs and cats to keep them alive, and then a few days later, they threw them in a pile, like they were garbage. It just didn't seem fair that all those beautiful dogs and cats never found anyone to love them, and take them home to be their pets, or take care of them. Only the lucky ones found homes. How could they do such a thing? I knew it was wrong to kill these animals. I could never do what they did. I'm only a kid, and what I thought wouldn't change anything.

Even though we didn't go as much, we did go to the ASPCA across the street. Now, when we looked into the cages, we were sad to think what would become of them. We knew that most of the dogs and cats wouldn't become someone's pet. Most of them had such a short time left to run around and nip at each other, as they barked playfully. I still sat at the gate and petted the dogs that came to me. Only now I stayed longer and tried to pet more of them. I knew this might be the last time I saw them, or that anyone touched them before they were gone … so a little extra kindness should be given to them. It was harder to say goodbye to them now. I didn't have to be home until dark, so I stayed until then.

Now when I left the big glass doors, I looked at the parking lot to see if there were any cars with parents and kids pulling in, looking to take home a new dog or cat. I hope this happened, and that they would all find homes. I wanted to remember them all with their eyes open, and their pink tongues ready to lick a waiting hand, wagging their tails and coming to the gate to find a new family.

The Silver Bullet

NEAR THE CORNER, to the right of my building, is Aldo's Dry Cleaners on Morris Park and Tremont Avenue. That's where The Silver Bullet stays. The Silver Bullet was silver, but it wasn't a bullet. The Silver Bullet was a 1957 Chevy four-door BelAir with big bench seats, roll-up windows, and an automatic transmission. My dad called it The Silver Bullet, although I never knew why. He loved this car and paid six hundred dollars for it. There was a black two-door coupe, the same year that he liked, but it was three hundred dollars more. Dad didn't have deep pockets, so The Silver Bullet came home with him. The Bullet sat in front of the building. It was a great car to lean against or sit on. The front fender was round and comfortable, but the rear fender couldn't be sat on; it was sharp and pointy-shaped, like a shark's fin. The doors were never locked, and it provided me and my friends with a comfortable clubhouse as well as a perfect hiding place for "hide and seek," since no one ever looked inside cars. The big bench seats were long enough that I could lie down across them, and not touch the other door with my feet. When it rained, The Silver Bullet clubhouse was dry. In the winter, it was warmer than outside, since it blocked the wind. Sometimes there were as many as seven kids in the car. We had only one rule in The Bullet, and that was that I was the boss. I decided who came in, and who stayed out. On weekdays when Dad worked, my father would check it before going upstairs to the apartment. So another rule was that we had to be out before five o'clock.

On Friday nights, my father would drop me off at Nanny's house for the weekend, so I got a chance to ride in it. The Silver Bullet actually moved, so it wasn't only a clubhouse, it was also a car. When Dad drove, I sat in the passenger's seat and watched him as he drove. There were a lot of things to do to convert the clubhouse into a moving car. Once the doors were shut, Dad pumped the pedal twice. He said, "Any more, and we'll flood it." I thought, *Does that mean that if he pumped one more time, water would come pouring into the car and drown us?* I was glad he never pumped three times. Then he took hold of the starter switch with his thumb and index finger; it was broken and he didn't need a key, he turned it to the right and the motor started. He kept his foot lightly on the gas, he said, "so it wouldn't stall out." With the motor on, we had to sit there while it warmed up. We sat there until Dad decided it wouldn't stall. He said, "If it stalls, it won't start again, because it gets flooded!" (Again, water coming into the car! I'm glad it didn't stall — how would I explain to Nanny, when I arrived at her house, how I got wet?)

The motor didn't stall. Now Dad rolled down the window and stuck his arm out. With his other hand, he moved a big stick next to the steering wheel toward the floor and it clicked into "D." The Bullet began to move. At the light we made a left on Tremont Avenue, and in about twenty minutes, we were at Nanny's house. At red lights, Dad moved his foot from the long pedal to the other square pedal. He called the square one "the brakes." I knew it was called the brakes because during the drive when he stepped on that pedal, he said, "The brakes squeak." Most Fridays this was what we did together. He drove me over to Nanny's house. When we got to Nanny's house, he didn't get out of the car to come upstairs to see Nanny or Granddad. Instead, I would run upstairs and wave out the window to him. He beeped The Silver Bullet's horn as he saw me wave; then he drove away. Some Fridays I would sit in The Silver Bullet and wait for my dad to get off the train and drive me to Nanny's house. When I waited too long, I would listen to the radio. I saw that when Dad turned the key switch to the right, two red lights went on in the dashboard and the radio would play, so I tried it, and it worked. When I played the radio, it didn't seem so long of a wait. Sometimes when I wasn't careful and pushed the car starter too far to the right, I could hear the motor almost start.

Soon, Dad got off the train and into the car. He pumped the gas twice, turned the key switch to the right, and the motor was on. He stuck his arm out the car window, and put the stick in "D," and we were on our way, like so many times before. Driving the car looked like fun, and it looked like I could do what Dad did—after all, I saw it done so many times, and I watched Dad's every movement. On Sunday nights when Granddad drove me back to the apartment, he did the same things as Dad did. So I thought Granddad showed Dad how to drive, and by watching Dad, he showed me how it was done, so.... I wanted to drive too.

Monday came and all day while I was in school, I pretended to drive: what I had to do, and how I was going to do it. In my head I went over all the things I saw Granddad and Dad do. The next Friday, when Dad drove drive me to Nanny's house, while sitting next to him I said, "Dad, I want to drive the car too."

Without hesitation, he said, "At the next light, jump in my lap and you can steer."

At the next light I jumped into his lap, and began to steer the car. I grabbed the steering wheel with two hands. My dad's hands were under mine, helping and guiding me as I steered the car. We did this week after week until he removed his hands from under mine, and just gave me orders: "stay straight," "turn left," and "turn right." Once in a while he had to grab the wheel to correct me. After a while I got better and better with the steering wheel, and Dad just worked the pedals and gave me steering orders. I felt the time was right and I could drive The Silver Bullet, but I couldn't reach the pedals. Since I spent so much time in The Bullet as a clubhouse, I knew that if you touched the side of the seat on the floor, there was a metal piece that moved the seat forward and backward. I moved the seat forward as much as it could go, but I still couldn't reach the pedals. When I got a haircut, the barber put two telephone books underneath me so he could cut my hair without bending over too much. When I sat at Nanny's table in the kitchen, she also put two telephone books underneath me, so I could reach the table and eat. So now that I decided to drive, I had to sit on two telephone books.

On the day I was going to drive, first I would have to go to Harry's candy store, go into to the phone booth, and get two telephone books. The phone books were always on the floor of the booth or right next to the door. I knew what I had to do; I had to get the phone books! My plan to drive was starting to get better. All day in school, all I could think about was driving, and I knew today was the day; I was confident and ready. On the bus ride home, I told my best friend Paulie about my plan. He was very excited, and said he wanted to come with me. We got off the bus and ran into Harry's candy store. Paulie went into the phone booth and came out with one telephone book. He tucked it under his arm with his other schoolbooks, and walked out without being noticed. Next, it was my turn, and I did it just like Paulie. We met outside the candy store with the phone books, and ran to The Silver Bullet. We laughed as we ran with the books in our hands. We looked around to see if anybody was watching us. We were in The Silver Bullet as a clubhouse so often that nobody paid attention to us.

We got into The Bullet and I slid over to the driver's seat. One by one we put the phonebooks underneath me and I got taller. Now I could see over the wheel to the street in front of me, but now because I was up higher, my legs were shorter, so I was farther away from the pedals. To drive The Bullet I had to come up with a way to get to the pedals. The only thing that came to me was that Paulie should sit in front of me, on the floor. He could work the pedals. All I had to do was tell him which pedal to push. With every problem solved, now it was time to drive.

With Paulie in position, I told him, "Push the long pedal two times and get off it." I turned the key switch to the right, and the motor started. Upon hearing this, Paulie and I were screaming with excitement.

"Paulie, hold down the long pedal just a little bit," I said, and he did. "Paulie, get off the pedal; I think the motor is warm now." I rolled down the window and put my arm out. I put the handle in "D" and The Bullet began to move forward slowly. There were no cars in front of us; we were in front of Aldo's Dry Cleaners next to the fire hydrant. I knew that Nanny's house was far away, and I didn't know how to get there, but I knew my neighborhood. I knew from riding my bike that if I turned right on Tremont Avenue and went down the street to Carlos' house , and then made a right turn at Andrew's house, and made another right turn on Lebanon Street, I went completely around the block, and I would be back in front of my building where we started from. Then I could put The Silver Bullet back in its spot. After all, I didn't want anyone to find out what we had done.

As we moved slowly forward, I looked for other cars, but there were none. I made a turn at the corner. We were moving really slowly, so I told Paulie to touch the long pedal. He pushed down on it really easy, and we were going a little faster now, down the block to Carlos' house. I said, "Paulie, push down the other one, the small one — that's the brake, and we'll slow down."

He did, so we slowed down and I turned The Bullet down to Andrew's house. Paulie lifted his head to look out the window, his eyes open wide, and his mouth open as he yelled, "We did it; we did it!" as he laughed really loudly. We were going slowly, barely moving forward; I was so excited, I forgot to tell Paulie to push down on the long pedal so we could go faster. I told Paulie, "We have to turn right onto Lebanon Street."

Paulie lifted himself up and looked out the window, yelling, "We're doing it, we're doing it!" We crept along slowly as Paulie didn't push down on the long pedal. At the corner, I pushed Paulie down to work the pedals.

"Push the small one and hold it," I said as I turned the corner onto Morris Park Avenue. We were rolling slowly toward the corner, to the same spot where we started from. I turned the wheel hard to the right, and told Paulie, "Push down on the small pedal and hold it." We hit the curb as Paulie pushed down on the pedal. We came to a bumpy stop when the front wheels hit the curb and pushed The Bullet back on onto the street. If the curb hadn't been there, we would have gone onto the sidewalk. After bouncing off the curb, somehow, we straightened out. Paulie was still on the floor holding the pedal when I took the handle and put the stick in "P." The Bullet came to a hard stop as our bodies jerked forward, but we did it!

I turned the key lock to the left, and the motor shut off. Paulie came up off the floor and looked at me; we both laughed until our stomachs hurt. We talked about our ride for a long time as we sat in the car. As we talked, we recalled every move we had each made, and how great it was. Even though we were excited about our ride, and couldn't believe it ourselves, we promised never to tell anyone, or we would both get in trouble. In our Bronx neighborhood, and the way we grew up, I knew we wouldn't be in trouble. It would probably never even get back to my father. We would be heroes. I could the kids say, "You did what?" We would be the talk of every kid on the block, even the big kids, and my friends' older brothers. Even at their age, it would be a long time before they could do what me and Paulie did.

We never took the phone books back to Harry's candy store. We were afraid Harry would see us coming in with the books and start asking questions. We ditched them in the garbage cans at the side of the building. Paulie and I always laughed when we thought about our ride. We laughed secretly with each other every time we said, "Remember when we...?" We didn't finish the sentence, and we both knew what the other one was going to say. We laughed until our bellies hurt. It's a shame we couldn't talk about it, and tell everybody, and be the heroes we really were — but after all, little kids like us shouldn't be driving cars. Even though we did, and we knew how.

D and D

IT WASN'T OFTEN that we did things together as a family. We weren't the type of family that you see on TV. That family lived on channel two, four, and seven, not in my house. That type of family that was portrayed on TV probably lived in the suburbs, not in The Bronx in an apartment building. *Father Knows Best* didn't live at my house. *Danny Thomas* or *Leave It to Beaver*-type families didn't exist in The Bronx tenements. Blue-collar dads worked, and mothers slept all day until the neighborhood bar opened — or at least mine did. On one Saturday night, me, Mom, and Dad got into the silver '57 Chevy BelAir (The Silver Bullet) and drove to Tremont Avenue and Parkchester to a fancy Chinese restaurant. We sat in a booth with a white tablecloth and had hot tea in small cups placed in front of us. I never had hot tea before, and with a lot of sugar and ice it became my new drink of choice. Dad ordered a Pu-Pu platter that had a small black iron cup in the middle that was on fire, and there were chunks of food placed around the fire in wooden bowls that sat on the bed of lettuce. All I could think of was what a thrill to have something to do as you ate; you heated up the bits of food before you ate them. There were chicken legs, spareribs, and meats on sticks, and cut up bite-sized eggrolls.

It felt strange to have all three of us at the same place at the same time, eating together. We took turns heating the meat sticks in the fire; we resembled cave people as we ate, and grunted after each bite. As the fire died out, and the bits of food were eaten, the waiter took away the empty platter, and brought out more food under silver trays. Under the silver-topped trays all the food was mushy with lots of vegetables. Until now, I'd only eaten hotdogs, hamburgers, sandwiches, food from Grandma Pearl's card games, and Nanny's Italian food. This Chinese food was very different. I wasn't sure if I liked it — everything tasted the same to me — but I did like putting the bits of food in the fire and eating that way.

As I looked around at the other booths and tables, I realized only the waiters were Chinese; everybody else was like us … not Chinese. Throughout the meal, we didn't talk much; Mom and Dad didn't have a word to say to each other. They acted like they didn't even like each other. When they spoke to me, they never spoke to me like I was a child. They spoke to me like I was one of them, their age. We didn't talk about school or friends or what I was up to. They had limited adult conversation that I was allowed to join in. We didn't talk or look like any of the families on TV. We didn't have the laughter after each thing we said; we had no laugh track or live audience giggling as we spoke.

After a while, the silver trays of food were eaten and empty. The waiter brought out ice cream and pineapple chunks for dessert without us even asking for it. As we ate dessert, Dad told Mom, "We're going to D and D."

I thought we were going out somewhere else after this dinner, so I repeated, "We're going to D and D?"

The both of them shook their heads and started to laugh. Mom said she had to go to the bathroom, and Dad said he would get the car, so "wait here until your mother gets out of the bathroom, and I'll meet you outside." There I was, sitting in the booth at the Chinese restaurant by myself, spooning out the last of the ice cream and pineapple chunks. Mom got out of the bathroom, walked rapidly over to me, grabbed my arm, and said, "Let's go now, let's go," with a real stern face as her head went back and forth, looking at the waiters. We walked out past the cashier, who was sitting behind the glass booth that had cookies and gum and colorful Chinese fans. Mom headed straight for the door while stepping so fast that she dragged me behind her as she held my arm. As she pushed open the door, the silver Chevy pulled up to the curb and came to a screeching stop; both doors opened up on our side. Mom pushed me into the back seat. The car door slammed closed behind me as she jumped into the front seat. Dad burned rubber as we sped away from the Chinese restaurant.

They were real quiet for a few minutes, and then they broke out in a few giggles — the giggles turned into big belly laughs. I too started to laugh, even though I didn't get the joke, or didn't hear anything funny that was said. I asked, "What's so funny?"

My mother said, "Don't tell him."

My father, in a deep slurring W.C. Fields voice, while holding a pretend cigar, said, "We pulled a D and D."

"Dad, what's a D and D?" I asked, again.

In the W.C. Fields voice, with his fingers holding an invisible cigar, he said, "We DINED, and we DASHED, and we didn't pay for the dinner."

Mom and Dad laughed — was it laughter because of the voice, a free meal, a night out, or all of the above? As I sat in the back seat looking at my parents getting along and laughing, Dad had his arm around Mom; it reminded me of a movie I saw. They were the Bonnie and Clyde of restaurants. They, like Bonnie and Clyde, were excited by what they just did, and now they had something to talk about. Even though what they did was wrong, for tonight they were getting along, and we were a happy family, for a bunch of petty criminals. I knew I could never do what they did that night. The D and D was so wrong. So I learned one thing that night: If you can't pay the bill, don't sit down and eat.

The Hood and the Fence

IT HAD BEEN snowing nonstop for two days. All the schools in The Bronx were closed. Today was officially a snow day. Yesterday, as the snow was falling, we played in front of Harry's candy store. My friends and I planned to meet in front of my building today to play in the snow if the schools were still closed. The snow was always deepest on my corner. The plow trucks had to remove the snow along bus routes — Tremont Avenue and Morris Park Avenue had to be cleared. All the snow from both avenues was pushed up in front of my building on the corner. There were eight of us who showed up to play in the snow. The first hour or so, we dug out holes in the front of the big snow piles. The snow piles were ten feet high, and deep enough to make Bronx-style igloos.

Once inside our frozen clubhouse, we chose sides and started packing snowballs for ammunition for the big snowball fight. The big snowball fight lasted only a few minutes. It took longer to make the snowballs than to throw them. A lot of snowballs were thrown, but just a few connected. Being bundled up in sweaters and coats, your throwing arm could barely move, so hitting your target wasn't easy. We were so bundled up that if you did get hit, no matter how big the snowball, you couldn't feel it.

After all the snowballs were gone, now what could we do with the snow? We walked down Lebanon Street, stopping to pack and throw a few snowballs at each other as we hid behind the parked cars that were covered with snow. The snow drifts were so high that the cars were completely covered, and it looked like a wall — a great white fortress wall. As we hid behind the walls of snow, the only way to score a hit was to lob it over the wall and hope it landed on someone's wool cap, since we couldn't see each other. We walked as far as the lots under the train trestle. There were always a few old abandoned cars there, so we continued our snowball fight, hiding behind the cars. We played behind a beat-up car that had no tires and a broken windshield. The doors and the hood were taken off and rusting a few feet from the car. It looked like someone took it apart and took out what they needed, and left the old rusting skeleton in the graveyard, like old dinosaur bones.

Me and Paulie walked over to the car hood and pushed it over and sat on top of it. The other kids pushed us a few feet, like we were on a sled, but it was heavy and difficult to move. Since there were eight of us, we all grabbed a corner of the hood and pushed it up a small hill that was the entrance to the lots. Once we reached the top of the hill, we all jumped on top of the hood for a short but fun ride, until we came to a slow stop. We all laughed about our car hood that we made into a sled. How cool it was that we could all fit on top of the hood and ride together! We each grabbed a corner of the hood, and did it again. Even though there were eight of us, the car hood was real heavy. We're just little kids, and the biggest one of us couldn't have weighed more than fifty or sixty pounds. It took a lot of work to pull and drag the car hood up the small hill, but we did, over and over again. All that work, and our ride was over so quickly.

My friend Donald said, "Let's drag this thing up the side of the highway near the bus stop, and get a real ride." We all agreed — that sounded like a great idea. A faster, longer ride was what we all wanted. When an idea was thrown out from one of us, the rest of the gang, wanting to fit in, went for it. You never wanted to be the kid that stood out, and not join in the fun and excitement.

This hill was so tall that when you were on top, you were as tall as the six-story buildings across the street. So we knew Donald was right and the ride down would be long and fast. At the bottom of the hill, there was a chain-link fence, so when the ride was over, we wouldn't go into the street and get hit by cars or buses, since this was Morris Park Avenue, and there was traffic.

We all carried the car hood up Lebanon Street. We looked like the seven dwarfs when they carried Snow White while she slept. We carried the hood across Morris Park Avenue and started our way up the side of the hill for the great ride down. For kids our size, it took every ounce of strength, pulling and pushing, to get the car hood to the top of the hill. No matter how hard we worked, we knew it would be worth it. When we reached the top of the hill and looked down, it felt like we had just climbed Mount Everest, and Lebanon Street looked like it was down in a valley. I got that same feeling in my stomach as the time I went to Rye Beach Playland and went on the roller coaster and looked down when I was on top — like someone was tickling my stomach from the inside. We all looked at each other and giggled with excitement. We said the same thing at different times: "Man, what a ride," as we pushed the car hood to the top of the hill.

We all wanted to ride in the front. I got real loud and I was the first one who called it, so somehow I convinced the other kids that I should sit in the front row. We had two in the front, three in the middle, and three in the back. All eight of us sat cross-legged on the top of the car hood. The kids on the outside pushed with their hands and feet to help us move forward a little, until the hill could take over. As we got closer to the edge and saw the steep hill, we all shouted: "One, two, three!" As kids, we all love to count things off. On three, the car hood with us sitting on top of it was off like a rocket! We never figured out between the car hood, our body weight, and a steep snow-covered hill, that we would fly down the hill as fast as we did. By the time we saw the bottom of the hill, we were there. We must've reached sixty miles per hour — with one problem. With the speed of the car hood sled, we weren't slowing down or stopping anytime soon.

The fence at the bottom of the hill stopped us. It was like we hit a brick wall. The back of the car hood went up in the air, as the front caught the bottom of the fence with all of us on it. The car hood was on top of us, pressing us against the fence. It looked like a big clam shell that closed up with us in it as it stood straight up against the fence. With the weight of the hood on top of us, we were pinned against the fence, like bugs that flew into a screen door. The two riders in the front — one of them was me — hit the hardest, right into the fence. I was like a cushion for the other kids, who were thrown forward on top of me. We were all piled on top of each other, like a loose football at a game when it hits the ground. There we were, all eight of us against the fence and on the ground, with the car hood on top of us. We'd planned the ride, but not how to stop! We hit so hard that the wind was knocked out of us.

All eight of us were crying and rolling around in pain. Frozen tears ran down our cheeks as the snow covered us. We all moaned and rolled around in the snow for what felt like forever as we tried to catch our breath. We were panting like puppies after a run. We were winded from the impact of hitting the fence and from deep belly crying. I was never hit by a truck, but this was what it must feel like. Such a sweet ride, such a bad ending. I'm sure no one wanted a second ride. We all cried as we limped across Morris Park Avenue. Since we were all crying, no one could be singled out and called a baby. We were all crying, but none of us were babies. Especially after what we just did. As I walked across the street in tears, that's when I figured out: Don't sit in the front of a ride unless you know how it's going to end!

We didn't talk to each other as we walked across Morris Park Avenue; there were only a few sniffles and out-of-breath sighs. One by one we walked into Harry's candy store and took napkins from the counter to dry eyes and blow noses. Since I had a tab at Harry's, I told his wife Florence to give us all hot chocolate — my treat. As we sat on the red stools and sipped hot chocolate, we were still trying to catch our breath.

The first one of us to talk was Donald. He said, "Maybe that wasn't such a good idea after all."

If there was ever a moment when a good friend should remain

silent, that was it. After a few sips of hot chocolate and cheeks that came back to room temperature, we started telling tales of the car hood and the hill that we had conquered. There we were — eight little liars, who forgot we had just dried our eyes and caught our breath a few moments ago. No one admitted to each other how banged up we were, but under those jeans and jackets were scrapes and black-and-blues. We left the car hood across the street, propped up against the fence as a monument to our ride. As we sipped our hot chocolate, in the comfort of Harry's, every once in a while, we looked across the street at the hill, and somehow, that hill didn't look so big anymore.

Secret Agent Boys

ON A SATURDAY, if you had a dollar, it was movie day all day. It was only fifty cents for the Saturday matinee at the movie theater under the train trestle at West Farms. The other fifty cents was for a soda, medium popcorn, and a Hershey bar. We — usually about five of us — would take a long walk from our neighborhood on Morris Park Avenue down Tremont Avenue into West Farms. The old lady in the glass booth, who looked like a fortune teller, gave you a ticket and fifty cents change when you gave her your dollar. When one movie ended, another one began, as we sat in our seats and threw popcorn at each other. By the time we walked home after watching all these movies, whatever we just saw was forgotten. All except today's one special movie. This was the movie that changed our lives. It was James Bond 007. Was there ever a man more slick, who could get in and out of trouble without a scratch? He drove cars, boats, airplanes, submarines, helicopters, and motorcycles. He shot guns and rockets and had secret gadgets to surprise his enemies and get him out of any sticky situation. Nothing could stop him, nothing could hurt him, and he was loved by the prettiest of ladies. He delivered microfilms in his wristwatch and secret plans that saved the world. He had a network of people that helped him, no matter where he was, in any country in the world. James Bond 007 — what a man.

By the time we left the movie, we all wanted to be James Bond 007, and live the life of danger and intrigue. As we walked home that day, we were convinced that the spy world was our future, and we were going to be secret agents. We gave ourselves numbers, all starting with 00, and we made up rules as we went along. We could no longer call each other by name for fear of losing our anonymity and being captured or killed! We had to carry weapons and bombs, and gadgets, and take orders, and go on missions to save the world. It was only natural that Harry's candy store was our headquarters. This was where we could meet and get our assignments for the mission of the day. At Harry's, we bought black hand guns that shot plastic pellets. We carried our pellet guns in our socks for protection against the bad guys. In our pockets we carried a book of matches in case we got captured and had to burn our way out, or start a fire to create a diversion so we could escape. When you're an agent, you have to be resourceful.

Now that we were agents, we had to dress differently. Long-sleeved shirts replaced our T-shirts. Long pants replaced our shorts. You can't hide a gun wearing shorts. The long-sleeved shirts hid the maps and assignments that were up our sleeves and held in place by rubber bands ... like no bad guy would check up our arms! We taped money to our rib cages under our shirts, in case we had to take buses while on assignment, or to pay off a spy, or make a phone call to another country. We taped up whatever change we had in our pockets; if we perspired, the tape didn't hold, so we had to keep our cool.

Our agency was so secret that the government wasn't funding us, so we didn't have the best of equipment. Like James Bond, we carried a pen that wasn't really a pen. When it was unscrewed, it was hollow and we filled it with chalk powder; in the right situation, it could be poured into an enemy's drink and they would be poisoned when they drank it, so we could get away. With the same powder, when you blew it in your enemy's face, it would blind them and you could escape any situation. In our pockets we kept plastic Easter eggs that split in the middle, which we filled with life-saving devices. One egg was filled with pebbles and last year's firecrackers; with that bomb, you could easily blow down a wall. Another egg was filled with Kool-Aid — poisoned Kool-Aid — which we could use against our enemies; or if our situation was hopeless, then we would have to drink it ourselves. The third egg was filled with marbles that could be thrown at the feet of our enemy as we watched them trip and fall to the ground. When you're secret agents like us, you must always be prepared and have an escape planned, since being captured could be fatal.

In our sneakers we hid maps of the block that we drew XX's on for drop points and secret meeting places where we could hide without being captured after an assignment. The abandoned lots on Lebanon Street were our safe area. A big X marked where the old burnt Chevy was. The thing about being a secret agent is that you must carry out your missions in secret. You can't be seen with the other agents. We passed each other on the sidewalk like we didn't know each other, and slipped each other notes and instructions for our next move. Here we were, Agents 001-006, protecting the world — none of us could be 007; that was reserved for James Bond. Even though he was one of us, and we worked with him, we never saw him. He was on bigger cases than we were, since he was more experienced.

The drop points were marked with stars. Today we were to pick up a shoebox filled with secret stuff that had been placed there by Andrew. Since he had his dad's old briefcase, and his hair was black and slicked straight back, he was our boss. In it may have only been a piece of old newspaper, or a bottle, or a baseball card, but they were all secret clues that had to be delivered and passed around to complete our mission. When our mission was complete, we were instructed to meet at the X (the old Chevy). That is, if we weren't captured or killed. Once we got to our rendezvous point, we told close call stories of being followed, and spies that almost got us, and our weapons and gadgets we used to get away. We opened up the shoebox full of secret stuff we collected on our mission. Here was where the experience comes in. We tried to figure out what it all meant. These items were clues, but not from our government or the bad guys. These were the clues that sparked our imaginations, our commitment to adventure, in the fraternity of "Secret Agent Boys." Tomorrow, there would be new assignments and new clues.

Keeping The Bronx safe from spies isn't easy. It takes hard work, and sharp agents like us. As long as we stick together, we can defeat evil, and the world is a better place.

School Days

THE ALARM CLOCK at the foot of my bed went off. It was seven o'clock. I crawled to the bottom of the bed with my eyes shut, and pushed down the button on the alarm. The clock is at the foot of my bed on a small night table that's inches from my parents' double bed. Dead asleep and motionless, Mom snores through the alarm. Her mouth half-open, and her eyes half-shut is how she sleeps. The room smells like a bar, since she was out drinking yesterday, and into the night. Unlike most mothers of a seven-year-old, she lies fast asleep, not anxious or concerned to get me off to school. I can do this by myself anyway, since I do this every day. On the table with the alarm clock, there are two crumpled dollar bills waiting for me. The two dollars were left by my father, before he went to work. On days when there was no money left for me on the table, then I charged our breakfast at Harry's candy store and luncheonette.

This morning, I went over to the old-fashioned steam radiator by the window to get my clothes. Yesterday after I got out of the shower, I draped them over the hot radiator with hopes they would be dry by morning. At three o'clock yesterday after school, I watched *The Three Stooges* on channel nine. Curly was in the shower fully dressed, soaping down his clothes and singing, so I tried it. How great was this — Curly, of The Three Stooges, taught me how to do laundry while I showered! The pants and shirt were dry, so I put them on. They felt warm, too. The only problem was that everything that dried on the radiator had lines on it in the same shape as the radiator — even my socks. The clothes were stiff, not soft like when Nanny did them on Friday nights when I slept over. At least they were clean. Tonight, when I showered before bed, I was going to take my dirty sweatshirt in with me, and give it a Curly wash.

I walked over to the nightstand and took the two dollars. I sat on my bed, and put my sneakers on. I glanced over, hoping to see my mother wake up or gesture to me to come over to her, but there was no movement as she lay there snoring. As I looked at her sleeping, she looked so peaceful. While she slept, she couldn't slur her words or smack me around for no reason, like when she was drunk. People said that she looked like Elizabeth Taylor. They said she had her eyes and her black hair, even though Mom's hair was dyed that color. At my age, I didn't know who that was. I was sure, though, whoever Elizabeth Taylor was, she was a better mother than mine.

I unlocked the door and closed it behind me — I didn't have a key yet, Dad said I was too young. I walked down the steps of our four-story apartment on Morris Park Avenue in The Bronx, and walked over to Harry's on the corner. I gave his wife Florence our breakfast order. The order was always the same: for Mom, one coffee, light and sweet, one French cruller, and one pack of Kool Kings 100s. For me, chocolate milk and a chocolate glazed doughnut, which I ate at the counter, while sitting on the red stool. Florence never looked up when I ordered or spoke to her. She had short, thick, curly black hair and a boxer's nose with a bump in the center. Her big manly hands worked rapidly like a robot's, as she placed the items in the brown paper bag. While I sat there eating, through the window I could see the other kids holding hands with their moms, starting to walk up to the school bus stop. I swallowed down the doughnut, hardly chewing, and drink the chocolate milk down fast, so I could run back to the apartment to drop off Mom's paper bag, and get my books. I had to hurry to catch the school bus — if I didn't get there in time I knew I would miss school, since Mom couldn't get me there.

I ran to the apartment building. Once inside, I always ran up the steps. I knew I could beat any elevator to save time, and catch my bus. Once inside the apartment, I put the paper bag with the coffee, cigarettes, and French cruller on the nightstand next to Mom while she slept. I took my books that were on the kitchen table from the night before, and ran out of the apartment, without saying goodbye to Mom, since she was still sleeping.

Even though I was usually the last one on the bus, at least I made it. As all the kids waved goodbye to their mothers and a few fathers, I waved at them too, since I knew most of them from the neighborhood. Most of the mothers knew me, too, and gave me a special wave goodbye, like I was one of their kids. As the school bus pulled away from our neighborhood, I couldn't wait to get to PS 105 and go to class. I also couldn't wait to get home from school and shower with my clothes on again. This time, I thought I'd sing in a high voice, like Curly...la leeeee, la laaaaa, la leeeee....

Free Lunch at School

FREE LUNCH AT school sounded like a good thing, unless it was you who were on that line while the other kids looked at you. Lunch at school was always edible, but never good. There were two choices: hot lunch or cold lunch. Hot lunch was a watery tomato soup with beans in it, and a cheese sandwich on white bread, and a small carton of milk. Cold lunch was the same cheese sandwich with a container of milk, without the soup. Not exactly fit for a king or a kid. Across from the free lunch side was the pay lunch side. It was 55 cents, and cake, cookies, or any dessert, even ice cream, was another 25 cents.

The pay side had older ladies with hair nets on their heads, who asked you what you wanted. The free side had everything already laid out on pink plastic trays that looked like it had been there since dinosaurs walked the earth. On the pay side, you had a lot of choices available — the ladies scooped up macaroni and cheese or spaghetti with meatballs. They had hotdogs and hamburgers with French fries. Every day the menu changed, so if you had 80 cents, you not only had a choice of what you could eat for lunch, you had something different every day. It was like a restaurant with self-serve pink tray delivery, instead of table service with waiters. At an early age, your school status was determined by what line you're in. What line you're in determined where and who you sit with for lunch.

I was already a bused-in kid, not a walker. The walkers lived near-by within a few blocks of the school. My school, Public School 105, was in Pelham Parkway in The Bronx, which is considered a good neighborhood, a lot better than mine. Most of the bused-in kids were also the free lunch kids, since we didn't come from areas as nice as Pelham Parkway and our parents didn't have the money they had. A few weeks before school started, my mother got a blue card in the mail from the school. It was a questionnaire that was sent out to all parents. On it was the bus number, and the pick-up and drop-off times for the school bus. She filled out the blue card. On it were my name, address, and telephone number in case of emergency — and she also checked the free lunch box.

With that box checked, I was condemned to be a free-lunch–bused-in kid, and in Pelham Parkway, that didn't spell "popular street." Not only did I have to ride the bus back and forth to school instead of walk, but everybody saw me in the free lunch line. The food was bad, and the other kids looking at me made it worse. The kids didn't want to sit with me when I got off the free lunch line. It meant I wasn't from around their neighborhood, and outsiders were treated like Indians at a cowboy convention. In the beginning of the school year, the bused-in-free-lunch crowd stayed together and ate at the same tables.

After a few weeks, we all made friends with our classmates, and a few brave Indians sat at the cowboy tables. It was then, after being in the same class with me for three years, that Robbie Disuke waved me over to his table to sit with him and his boys. Most of the boys weren't too happy I joined them, but Robbie was the biggest, toughest third-grader in history, and he set the rules on who sat where. He was already as big as any full-grown man. He was the tallest kid in our whole school, even the sixth-graders. Robbie was as big a clown as he was a big tough guy. When he was in class, he did everything wrong — he laughed when he shouldn't have, and threw pencils and papers across the room. Whenever the teacher turned her back, somebody got slapped in the back of the head by Robbie. Every day he did something to send him to the principal's office. Even when he was trying to be good, he talked back to the teacher and disrupted the class by making strange loud noises like a wounded animal. He had the kind of laugh that when I heard it, I joined in and had to laugh along with him.

About every third visit to the principal's office, I kept him company, since I got in trouble for laughing at him. On the way to the principal's office, we first stopped into the boys' bathroom. I peed, he plundered. Robbie did every bad thing you could do, before and after peeing. He took paper towels and jammed them into the sink and ran the water, so the water would overflow onto the floor. He stuffed complete rolls of toilet paper down the toilet and flushed, until they too overflowed. He took the hand soap and mixed it with water and smeared it all over the mirrors. Somehow, he spelled every dirty word correctly.... While all this was going on, I became his audience. The more I laughed the more bad things he did. Robbie jumped on top of the bathroom stalls, and hung there like King Kong on top of the Empire State building. He kicked the walls and left his wet footprints everywhere. He turned over the garbage pails and spilled out the paper towels on the wet floor. Before we left the bathroom, his parting gift to the custodian was to take paper towels, wet them, and throw them at the ceiling, where they stuck there like mud pies. He was like a tornado at a trailer park, breaking and damaging everything in his path. I watched him come up with every bad idea since grammar school was created.

The more I watched him, the more outrageous he got. I didn't stop him, even though I knew it was wrong. I was afraid if I said something, it would be like in "Jack and the Beanstalk." I could hear this big giant of a boy as he came for me, with his arms stretched out in front of him: "Fe-Fi-Fo-Fum ... I'm going to get you, you little tattletale bum." He was that big! There was another reason I couldn't stop him ... he had pulled me off of the free lunch line. As the water flowed out of every sink and toilet, we made our way to the principal's office for our punishment.

Robbie was a frequent visitor to the principal's office, so he knew the slowest route to get there. That route also had to pass the lunchroom, which was now closed. Being a big kid, he ate a lot and he was always hungry. He walked into the closed lunchroom, and I followed.

He told me he was going to get some scooter pies and milk. With the stealth of the jewel thief, he wrapped his big arms around the entire crate of scooter pies and instructed me to put the box of milk containers on top of the scooter pies. We walked out of the lunchroom with the crate of scooter pies and a box of milk containers that could feed about fifty kids. We walked down the hall giggling, until a teacher saw us and called to us. In a stern voice, she almost yelled at us, "Boys, boys — stop right now; don't take another step."

The sternness of her voice made us stop like we were at a railroad crossing and we just saw the train. Now I knew we were in bigger trouble than before, and the bathroom flood had yet to be discovered.

She said, "Where are you boys going?"

Without hesitation, with Robbie's sincere, unblinking blue eyes, and perfectly combed blond hair, he said, "We're getting snacks for our class, and Ronald is helping, opening up the doors for me."

Robbie was a polished, talented con man, and at eight years old, and I was his nervous Barney Fife accomplice. With a delivery like that, the teacher, being satisfied, told us to carry on. We walked away holding back our giggles, and hid behind the staircase down the hall. Once there, we burst out laughing so hard that a few nose snorts snuck out. Robbie had his arm resting on the case of scooter pies like a hungry lion on a lifeless gazelle. We inhaled scooter pies and drank the milk. After six scooter pies and a pile of little milk containers on the floor, Robbie let out the loudest burp I ever heard. It didn't sound human. It sounded like a car horn. I knew our journey to the principal's office was inevitable, even though we had made a few detours. We walked down the hall shameless and giggling, with a few burps here and there. We reached the principal's office and sat on a big wooden bench in front of the closed door with his name on it in gold letters.

A few minutes passed, and Mr. Stark came out. He looked at us sternly and said, "Just sit there, if you can't behave in class."

What he didn't know was that we also couldn't behave in the boys' bathroom or the lunchroom. If we ever did get caught, I would never tell on Robbie. He was dangerously exciting, and fun to be with — and after all, he was the one who pulled me off the free lunch line. By doing so, Robbie changed my identity. I wasn't a bused-in-free lunch kid anymore. Thanks to Robbie, I was just one of the boys.

Kennedy Is Shot

I WAS SITTING in my classroom at P.S.105 in The Bronx; it was like every other day. Our teacher, Mrs. Lombardo, is writing on the blackboard, going over the answers to last night's math homework. Every time Mrs. Lombardo turns around to write something on the blackboard, a crumpled piece of paper flies across the room, followed by giggles. The more she writes, the more paper snowballs get tossed. It's always the boys. The girls sit quietly and pay attention to the teacher. Any opportunity boys are given to be bad is never overlooked in the classroom. As we sit in our chairs, we hear three tones that sound like a xylophone coming through the loudspeaker at the front of the room. We are all trained — when we hear those tones, it's an official announcement from our school's principal. Everyone, including our teacher, stops whatever they're doing and listens to the upcoming announcement.

"This is your principal, Joseph F. Stark speaking; I regret to inform you that the president of the United States has been shot. Your president, John F. Kennedy, has been assassinated; there will be an early dismissal. Boys and girls prepare for an early dismissal, and God bless us all."

He spoke very slowly, and in a deeper voice than usual. Our teacher, Mrs. Lombardo, put her hands on her face upon hearing this and cried. All of us, seeing our beloved teacher crying, knew this was very serious, and one by one we looked around the room, put our hands to our faces, and began to cry. I'm just a kid, so hearing about a man I don't know, a president, and that he's shot, and that word, assassination … I couldn't understand what was going on. When I looked to my left, Andrea was crying. When I looked to my right, Philip was crying. All of my classmates in front of me and behind me, and all across the room, were crying. As I sat there, I started to feel what they felt. I tried to hold back my tears, but I couldn't. I cried, too.

As I looked around the room, all thirty-three of us, my whole class, was crying. Somehow I felt the strength of their grief, and it surrounded me, like a painful hug. My thoughts were not mine, but theirs — the grief of all these kids, sharing the same emotion. The power of our sadness was so contagious that every kid in the class was crying. What a strong emotion we shared! We didn't all laugh at the same time, or at the same things, so why did we all cry at the same time? We all felt sad together; that united us. For the first time we were more than just classmates. We touched each other in a way we never had before. We were unanimous in our sadness, and all reduced to tears, and none of us felt embarrassed by it.

Our teacher went into her purse for a tissue and dabbed at her eyes and runny nose. She pulled out a box of tissues that was in her desk and offered it to us as we got out of our seats and crowded around her. She held out the box of tissues, and her hands were shaking. We wiped our eyes and blew our noses quietly. The girls were hugging each other in support of their sadness. The boys looked embarrassed as we turned away from each other with tears in our eyes. We didn't want to be seen crying in front of the class. Boys are not supposed to cry in front of each other. We are supposed to be stronger than the girls, but not this time.

Our teacher got down on one knee and put her arms out to as many of us as could fit inside. She said, "He was such a great man — how could this happen? Now what will we do without him? There has never been a president like him before."

She spoke of the president as if she knew him personally, as she dried her eyes with a crumpled wet tissue. Over the loudspeaker, the dismissal bell rang. The first bell was for the bused-in kids like me to make our way down the hall and out of the school to get on the bus. As I walked through the halls and looked inside other classrooms, they looked just like mine. Everyone was upset and crying as we were being released early from school. Everything felt different now that our president was dead. I boarded the school bus and we rode down Lydig Avenue. There were people in the street walking around looking confused and unhappy after hearing the terrible news of our president's death.

Today started out like every other day, but ended so differently from any other day. Sadness filled the air like dark clouds before a storm. I didn't fully understand how the loss of one man could sadden an entire country, but it did. Last year when my great- grandfather died, only my family cried; no one else shared our sadness. Our president must have been very special to have everyone in America feel such sadness and loss. Like everyone else, I couldn't smile or act like a kid right now. I felt what everyone felt. We all feel bad together. I didn't even feel bad for crying — today we all cried.

Jump Ropes and Hula Hoops

SINCE I WAS Marie's little boyfriend, when there were no boys around, I would play with the girls on the block. I was accepted by the girls because Marie said so, and nobody went against Marie. Marie was a head taller than all the other girls, and could be aggressive if she didn't get her way. She was the self-appointed leader of the pack. When I was with the boys, we played stickball, box ball, and football; we flew balsa wood glider airplanes; we played with yo-yos, we spun tops … the list was endless, what boys could do. At seven years old, I thought girls didn't have much of a variety of playthings or games. The girls were too old for dolls. Since we were outside playing, we had to play outdoor games. The games the girls played were jump rope and Hula Hoops.

Jump rope had lots of variations. There were the standard one-person jumps, and there were turners of the rope on each side. The jumper could also call in another one or two jumpers, and all the girls jumped together. When things got too easy, a second rope was added. The girls called this "Double Dutch." With Double Dutch you had to jump twice as fast because the second rope was coming right behind the first rope overhead. The rope turners had to have good rhythm, or the jumpers wouldn't last too long before the rope hit them in the ankle, and they were out. The turners looked like they were dancing in Double Dutch. They had a rope in their left hand, and a rope in the right-hand, and their shoulders swayed back and forth as they turned the rope. The rope turner on the opposite side did the same; they looked like dancing partners.

I never made it to Double Dutch. I was content and barely competent with single jump rope. The girls were fun to watch and light on their feet. They had more rhythm skills and weren't clumsy like the boys. Sometimes when they would jump rope, they would accompany it with a song or rhyme, like "John Jacob Jingle Hymer Schmitt." They would speed up the song and the jumper had to speed up her footwork. If the jumper couldn't clear the rope, and the rope touched any part of her body, she was out. Then the girl who was out became a turner — that's how the game was played. It was then I noticed that the girls could sing better than the boys, and they had more rhythm than the boys. Boys and girls were not created equal. When I jumped rope, the outcome was the same: get hit in the head as a rope turned, or have the rope trip me as it wrapped around my ankle. I never hung in there very long, and when I did wipe out, Marie gave the girls a *Don't laugh at him* stare, which spared me embarrassment.

When the girls got tired of jump rope, the Hula Hoops came out. Again I saw the difference between boys and girls. The girls rotated their hips with ease and moved the hoop over and over, spinning around without having it fall off their hips. They flowed smoothly, like water over a rock. With me, the rock was too big, or the hoop was too small — nothing flowed around my hips; it just fell to the ground after one circle. The girls were so good at it; they would see who could Hula Hoop the longest before it would hit the ground. No matter how I tried, I couldn't go more than one or two circles around my clumsy, no-rhythm body. For some reason this didn't bother me, since I thought this was a girl's game anyway, and I didn't have to be any good at it.

As the Hula Hoop lay on the ground at my feet, I couldn't wait to see another boy I could play with. I wanted to excel in something other than these girly games that I obviously wasn't built for. I thought about it, how at such a young age the girls were so fluidly agile, and I, a boy, so poorly built that I couldn't jump rope or Hula Hoop. As I thought about it, I realized it was just the nature of it all. Why fight it? These hips weren't meant to swivel, but these arms could throw a ball, and swing a bat better than any of the girls. With my new- found observation, that boys and girls were not created equal, I was comforted, and gave up jump rope and Hula Hoops. Marie wasn't happy that I stopped playing with her and her girlfriends.

It was also a good thing that no boys saw me playing with the girls. Tomorrow, if I didn't see any boys to play with, if I let Marie kiss me enough, I could talk her into playing hide and seek. Now there's a game that boys and girls could both play without rhythm or dancing hips. So tomorrow, when I got off the school bus, I'd go into Harry's candy store and buy Marie Juicy Fruit gum, and pucker up, and hope she couldn't resist me.

Roy Rubino

ON EVERY BLOCK in every neighborhood, there was always one kid who was a little chubby, or walked funny, or had a bad haircut, or a high voice. You didn't have to have much of a disability to be singled out and picked on. On Tremont and Morris Park Avenues in The Bronx, our lamb for the lions was Roy Rubino. He had it all. He was the lottery winner of victims. Roy was short, chubby, had an uneven crew cut, a large hooked nose, two broken front teeth, big ears, a protruding always bloody lower lip, crazy eyes — and when he ran, he tripped over his right leg, which was pitched in like a front tire that needed an alignment. On top of all this, when he got excited his voice went up a few octaves higher than any girl's, and when he spoke, he mispronounced every other word. I enjoyed playing with Roy; he was a lot of fun, and he could be talked into anything. That was what made him so popular.

One day while walking home from school, the older boys grabbed him. Each kid lifted him off the ground, by holding Roy under his armpits and grabbing on to his wrists with the other hand. He struggled a bit, but the boys had him off the ground, and as they walked him into the lots, the closer he got, the higher his voice became, and his words all came out wrong, from excitement mixed with fear. Once there, as everybody looked on — and by now, there were about a dozen kids — the boys filled his pockets with dog shit. Once his pockets were full they dropped him, and Roy ran home crying, as we all laughed cautiously. We, being the smaller kids, Roy's age, were afraid if we laughed too hard, the big kids would grab us, and do a Roy job on us too. Even though this was cruel, the reality was if you can't beat 'em, join 'em. Roy was our friend, but who wanted to suffer the same fate as Roy?

Another "get Roy day" wasn't far away, and soon it came. When we were tired of stickball, and box ball, and our usual games, we would go into the lots on Lebanon Street. We set up cans and threw rocks at the cans to knock them down, like target practice in the old Western movies. After a few games of hit the can, somehow we talked Roy into being a human target. We convinced him to sit on the concrete slab about thirty feet away from us, so we could throw rocks at him. Roy got hit with a few rocks we threw, but nothing really hit him hard enough to make him stop playing the game. A few more rocks and a few more hits, and Roy wanted some protection so he wouldn't get hit in the face. He got off the concrete target range area and walked off and came back with a cardboard box. He sat back on top of the concrete target area, and put his head inside the box to protect his face as we threw the rocks. Roy's plan worked well; if we were lucky enough to hit him with the rocks, his head was protected; the box worked like a football helmet or goalie's mask.

Roy had outsmarted us! Or so he thought. The only thing that Roy didn't think of was that now with his head in the box, he couldn't see us. That presented a challenge: the challenge was to penetrate Roy's armor, so the rocks got bigger and bigger, and we threw harder and harder, and we got closer and closer. He couldn't see us, so he didn't know how close we were, and how big the rocks got. Roy's plan was working well, until one of the kids got real close and had a rock the size of a grapefruit and.... Bang! A direct hit to the center of the box. The box slammed forward onto Roy's head with such tremendous force that it dented the box, and Roy's face behind it as well. Under that box was a bloody mess. Immediately upon the impact, Roy flung the box off his head and ran out of the lots. As he ran, his high voice was excitedly higher, he sounded like a Munchkin in *The Wizard of Oz*, on helium. He tripped as he ran; he was too excited to adjust his right leg that pitched inward. As he ran screaming, all his words were unrecognizable, he sounded like he was speaking another language. We all watched Roy, as he ran, tripped and screamed, holding his bloody nose. We all laughed so hard, one kid peed a little in his pants. Nobody ran after Roy; we knew Roy would be okay. The next day, no matter what you did to Roy, he was always okay and back for more. Roy loved to play, and we loved to play with him. That was Roy's appeal, that's what made him such a popular kid on the block. That…. And we knew that Roy could be talked into anything.

Yellow Sunglasses

THEY STEPPED OFF the plane and walked down the catwalk toward us. They looked so out of place. They looked like they were walking down the red carpet on Oscar night in Hollywood, waiting for photographers to snap their picture. Not only did their shirts and blouses match their pants, they even matched each other. Aunt Alice wore a yellow paisley print blouse with bright yellow slacks that stopped midcalf. She had yellow patent leather sandals with a big plastic daisy in the middle, and yellow painted toenails. Her hair was perfectly in place, held together with a big yellow daisy clip. She wore ruby red lipstick, and on her nose were the biggest pair of yellow sunglasses I ever saw. The yellow sunglasses were so big that it made her pronounced features seem small.

Her sons, my cousins, Billy and Richie, were beside her holding hands as they walked. They wore yellow-and-white-striped button-down collared shirts and yellow pants with brown penny loafers, complete with shiny new pennies in the middle. The boys looked like little golfers. Didn't they know this was New York, and nobody looked like this? They looked so out of town, they looked like they came from another planet. Even on television, I never saw people that looked like this.

Aunt Alice was my father's older sister. He was the youngest of his family. As they approached Nanny, Granddad, and me, I braced myself for the huge hugs and air kisses Aunt Alice always gave me when she visited. Her kisses never connected with my cheek, but she made that kiss sound anyway, as she closed her eyes and puckered up.

Aunt Alice lived in Fort Lauderdale, Florida. She moved out of New York about fifteen years ago after she got married to her husband, Uncle Bill. Uncle Bill was what my granddad called "a big shot." Granddad said he was a big shot in Southern Bell Telephone, and by our standards they were rich. They were the first people in our family to relocate, and own a house and a swimming pool, and have new cars. They even went on family vacations together. Boys being boys, when I saw Billy and Richie, we just shook hands, too uncomfortable to hug. As I shook their hands to greet them, they looked me up and down, and I always looked like a poor Bronx kid. A poster boy for the Fresh Air Fund. Compared to them, I was. They looked like a page out of a Sears catalog for children's clothing. I wore old blue jeans, a white T-shirt, and worn-out high top Converse sneakers. My outfit never matched and never changed. After we exchanged hugs and kisses, we all walked out of the airport, and waited curbside with their suitcases, while Granddad got the old black-and-white Chevy to drive us back to Nanny's apartment on Crosby Avenue in The Bronx.

This was Aunt Alice's yearly visit to see her parents. She and the boys usually stayed for two weeks. During their visit I also stayed at Nanny's house, since having Aunt Alice and the boys was our family's only major event. As Granddad pulled up with his car, Aunt Alice said, "Oh Mama, look at this old poop of a car — when are you going to get a new one?"

I knew from her other visits that Aunt Alice had a way of saying things and making Nanny feel uncomfortable, even though she was her daughter. She said things that reminded Nanny that our life here wasn't all that great. Aunt Alice drove a new Thunderbird, and you could see the old Chevy was beneath her, but it was her transportation, and no matter what degrading scenarios awaited her, she would be back in sunny Florida in a few weeks. The car ride to Nanny's was chatty, and Aunt Alice smiled and made such a fuss over me. She told me about the presents she had bought me, and I pretended to be excited, but it was always clothes, Floridian clothes. Paisley and pastel-colored clothes that I could never wear in The Bronx. Not unless I wanted to get beat up.

When we arrived at Crosby Avenue, Aunt Alice looked around as she stepped out of the car. She looked like a soldier that was about to step on a landmine. She said, "Nothing has changed — it's still dirty New York." She said the neighborhood looked the same as when she grew up in it. She didn't find it comforting to be back home where she grew up. She found it beneath her now. The boys, Billy and Richie, were trapped in the apartment. Aunt Alice slept in Nanny's bedroom, and the boys slept in the living room on noisy old aluminum cots with me. For them, there was no yard, no pool, no French poodle named "Frenchie" to play with. They thought they were being punished, compared to how they lived in Florida. This visit to New York was necessary, so when they got home they would appreciate all they had. This was a humbling experience for two little boys, to see how other people lived. It was the only time they ever walked up stairs.

During their visit, we mostly watched television. On the weekend we went to a pool in New Jersey called Idlewild, which was just over the George Washington Bridge. We also went to a state park in Connecticut and had a barbecue, and swam all day in Long Island Sound. For me, it was such a treat; it was my vacation. I didn't get to do these things all the time — only when Aunt Alice came to visit. During the week, Nanny and Granddad took us to an amusement park called Freedomland. Freedomland had rides and miniature golf and storybook settings throughout the park that came to life. As we walked through the park, Billy and Richie went through the blocking rope and joined in on a few scenes. Richie took a broom out of an elf's hands and started sweeping like a mechanical figure. On the next scene, Billy sat at a small desk with Benjamin Franklin, and put on his glasses and took his pen then pretended to sign The Declaration of Independence. We all laughed as these two well-behaved kids broke some rules for the sake of a good time.

A few days later, we went to Orchard Beach. Orchard Beach was a small beach located between Pelham Bay Park and City Island.

People who lived in The Bronx and knew Orchard Beach didn't call it Orchard Beach. It was always low tide and smelled horrible, so it was called "Horseshit Beach." On the day we went, it was stinky as usual. Aunt Alice pinched in her nose with her fingers to block the smell as we walked through the parking lot toward the beach. She wore a big straw hat, big yellow sunglasses, a colorful paisley blouse, and white pants she called "culottes." When we reached the sand, she said the smell was getting worse. Low tide was in full bloom. It probably went against nature's design, but I don't think that beach ever had a high tide. Me, Nanny, and Granddad were familiar with that smell. It wasn't exactly like walking into a bakery, but we weren't offended by it. We knew the trade-off would be to cool down in the water.

Nanny and Granddad spread out an old blanket in the sand. We brought coolers with sandwiches and fruit, and a big jug of red Kool-Aid. Me, Billy, and Richie headed for the water. Even though we were surrounded by water, Horseshit Beach wasn't a dangerous place for kids who couldn't swim. The only terrible thing that could happen to a kid was collapsing from exhaustion looking for deeper water as you walked in the water that started at your ankles, and no matter how far you went out, it never got past your waist. For some reason, that beach had no water. You couldn't swim in it even if you knew how to swim. It was that shallow. Aunt Alice said, "The water is too dirty to go in." So she stayed on the old blanket with Nanny and Granddad. I liked it, and the boys liked it, but it wasn't Fort Lauderdale Beach.

Seeing Aunt Alice and being with the boys was great for me, since I got a chance to be with my cousins who were so close to my age. Billy was a year younger than me, and it was nice to have him for a playmate, since I didn't have any brothers or sisters. Richie was three years younger than me, so for two weeks a year it felt like I had brothers, and was part of a family. During their visit, Aunt Alice paid a lot of attention to me. She was very sweet and affectionate. She was so unlike my mother. She was loving and caring to her children. She could see in my eyes, by the way I studied her, that I wished she was my mother. She knew my mother and the life I had, and that I was always with Nanny. She told me beautiful stories about Florida that filled my head with hope — how warm and wonderful it was, and the things they did together as a family. The big house, and the swimming pool that they enjoyed so much. She said she wanted to take me to live with her and go to school there. She said I would have a whole new life, a real family, and have Billy and Richie for brothers. At the end of her visit, like the ones before, I thought to myself, *Is this the one?* Would she find me so irresistible, that there would be an airplane ticket for me to go to Florida with her to start my new life?

The boys and I were up early watching television in the living room on the cots that we slept on overnight. Nanny was at the kitchen table having coffee, and putting on her makeup in her little round magnifying mirror. Soon the door from the bedroom opened, and Aunt Alice stepped out, looking already fabulous at nine o'clock in the morning. Her outfit, her hair, and her makeup were just perfect, and of course everything matched. She looked like a mom on television. She stopped into the living room to smother us with good morning kisses, as she went into the kitchen to join Nanny for coffee. As we watched cartoons, I also listened to Nanny and Aunt Alice in the kitchen, talking. Every sentence began with "Oh, Mama," followed by "You still have…" or "It's still broken…" and ended with a heartfelt laugh as they held hands. Aunt Alice knew this apartment well. She was a little girl when they moved in to the apartment on Crosby Avenue. The apartment was small, and had cracks in the ceiling and cracks in the walls, and needed painting and new linoleum floors. Even the furniture was the same as she remembered when she left the apartment and got married fifteen years ago. Even though Aunt Alice laughed, and pointed out what was old and damaged in the apartment, Nanny didn't get angry or embarrassed. She was just so happy that her daughter Alice had a better life than she did, and lived in a beautiful home and had nice furniture.

Nanny was proud of her daughter Alice, and nothing Alice could say could erase the joy she felt when they were together. She was the child who made it. She made it out of The Bronx, and had a successful husband, and kids who had everything. As Nanny put it, "they had a nice life." My father, and his other sister Ann, still lived in one-bedroom apartments in The Bronx, just getting by, with not much of a future. Moving to Florida and buying a home was never a thought in our lives. We were what we were, just getting by. Aunt Alice had a certain charm about her. When you were with her, you thought you were the only person that occupied her heart, and she truly loved you so deeply that she couldn't live without you. She had those glowing eyes of sincerity, like the nuns at Saint Theresa's church, where I went for Sunday Mass. She had that kind of face, and a smile like the keys on a piano, that made every bad thing go away. When she looked at you, she reached inside your heart to a gentle place, and made you feel good about yourself. She made you feel important to her. When she spoke to you, she would hold your hands gently in hers to confirm her passion.

Even though she genuinely did care for me, she never took me back home with her to Florida, so I could have the better life that she spoke of. I knew in my heart I didn't fit into her life. I was just her brother's kid, but for two weeks a year, she coddled, I dreamed, and in the end, we both were who we were before her trip to New York. During their visit, I dreamed of going home with them, but it never happened. I was hopeful till the end that they would take me with them. Even as we arrived at the airport, and the car door opened to let them out, I waited for a signal, for her to wave to me with her hand, "Come on, let's go." When the car door closed and I was still inside, I knew this year, like the others, she wasn't taking me back with her.

I watched Aunt Alice and the boys as they held hands and walked up the ramp of the airplane terminal. They turned and waved a few times. As the distance between us grew, the only thing recognizable was Aunt Alice's big yellow sunglasses. On the drive back to the apartment, we went over the Whitestone Bridge. We saw a plane overhead, and Granddad said, "Look and wave — that's Alice's plane. She should be home in a few hours."

Me, Nanny, and Granddad, driving the old black-and-white

Chevy, were at the apartment in a few minutes. I never did get to go to Florida, but for those few weeks, it supplied me with pastel fantasies and pants to match. My old blue jeans and white t-shirt probably wouldn't have fit in anyway. The thought of leaving The Bronx and having a real family faded, as soon as I sat in the apartment. Nanny and Granddad snored on the couch, with the loud television playing. I thought Aunt Alice was lucky, but I was lucky too, I have all this.... Hey, I'm just a kid, and I couldn't miss what Aunt Alice promised me, especially if I heard the same promise every year, and nothing came of it. When I saw Aunt Alice next year, and she told me about Florida, and how she's going to take me with her, I'd still open my eyes wide with excitement... and smile till it hurt. I had a whole year to practice that face in the mirror.... Maybe next year...or the one after that!!!

Roof Jumping

LEBANON STREET IN The Bronx where I lived was a landscape of apartment buildings. They're all tall buildings, six stories high. On the very top of these buildings, like all buildings, there's a roof. In the city a roof does more than keep the sixth floor dry. All the kids on the block were familiar with roofs. The roofs were a place we went up to fetch our Spaldeens when we played stickball. The roofs on either side of Lebanon Street were considered a foul ball, since the ball couldn't be fielded. These were street rules. When the ball was hit on the roof, the hitter had to go up and get it. The game got slowed down when the ball went on the roof, so the other option was to give up one of the balls in your pocket, since you carried at least three. Balls were like camels in the desert — bought, sold or traded, like cash. Every kid on the block filled his pockets with pink Spalding balls (Bronx pronunciation ... Spaldeen).It was a measure of wealth the more you carried. At the end of the game, the hitters had to go fetch all the foul balls that landed on the roof. Another function of the roof: when it was winter and cold outside, it was always warmest up there, since the sun wasn't blocked by the tall buildings that cast shadows on the streets below. Then spring came, and when we weren't playing in the street or at the lots, we went up on the roof to play. It was warmer than the street, and a little more comfortable.

As the spring changed to summer, the roof became what city people call "Tar Beach." That was when people from the building would strip down and go up on the roof in bathing suits to tan, and enjoy being outdoors after being cooped up all winter. We were creative on Tar Beach. We brought up small transistor radios and coolers with ice for our Yoo-Hoos, Cokes, and frozen Baby Ruths. Without going on a bus, we captured a small slice of the beach, without the sand between our toes. Some people brought beach chairs and blankets to lie out on "Tar Beach." They brought wash basins filled with cold water to soak their feet. Others kept a towel dunked in the cool water, which became a hat to escape the hot sun when there was no breeze. In the summer, there were times on the roof when it was so hot that the tar would melt under your feet as you walked on it.

The roof also sparked romance, as it became a make-out spot for the teenagers. They went on the roof to sneak a quiet kiss and some promiscuous petting. Sometimes we watched from a distance as we spied on the young couples. That was our first exposure to sex education. The roof also turned into a bar when the teenagers went up there to drink beer. It was parent-free, and "proof" was not required. Unfortunately, for some, the roof also became a drug area. They thought it was cool, when they were "high," to gaze at the stars at night, and during the day, to "get high" and sleep the day away, before the working parents got home. Those were the teenagers who experimented with pot and "huffing glue" on the roof.

The roof was many things to many people in the city who lived in the apartments below. We were all cramped in small apartments, and most of us lacked bus fare to get anywhere else. The roof provided a buffet of choices for an afternoon or evening, just by being there. Me, Paulie, Donald, Kevin, and a few other kids played hide and seek up on the roof. The clever players, who knew the roof well, seldom got caught. They touched home base while you were still out looking for them — the roof was that big. My roof took up half a block, so there were so many great hiding places. It wasn't long before we ventured to every corner of my roof, to all ends of the building. Like Columbus, who discovered that the world was not flat, we discovered that all the buildings that made up our entire block were connected. At the end of one building, another one was joined. Even though they were connected, the roofs didn't line up exactly with each other. Some were just a few feet different in height, while some were six or eight feet higher or lower, depending on where they were connected.

Once we discovered that the roofs were connected, we lost our fear of falling off, as long as we knew the difference from the connected side of the roof, and the non- connected side, to the street below. With our new-found knowledge, we started jumping from roof to roof, building to building. Like trained horses, jumping over fence hurdles, we ran and jumped from one roof to the next. Sometimes we started off on one roof, and exited from another building if the roofs didn't line up, and it was too steep to climb back after we jumped. Like young cubs in the jungle, once we became comfortable, it became our playground, off the ground.

Not all the kids on the block went up on the roofs and played on them. Some kids were scared, or were never introduced to the ways of the roof. Sometimes when we were at Harry's candy store, Me, Paulie, Donald, and Kevin would meet up with a kid who was new to the roof, so we told him the games we played up there, and how cool it was. We called these kids "roof newbies." When the newly recruited "roof newbies" went up on the roof with us, our goal was not to play hide and seek or jump roofs. They — the" roof newbies" — were to become our entertainment. Our goal was to "scare the hell out of them," while we were up on the roof. Our plan was to get the unsuspecting roof newbie to get where one roof ends and one roof began, where they were joined together. We then showed the newbies how brave we were.

Today, Donald was the star of the show. Donald pretended to walk along the edge of the roof, defying the plunge below. Since the newbies didn't know the roofs were joined, they watched reluctantly as Donald fearlessly cheated death. We worked as a team to frighten the newbies. It was like putting on a play. Donald walked the ledge, and the other three of us stood by the newbie. We yelled and acted excited as the ledge walker stumbled. After a few close calls, "Get down, you're gonna fall and get killed!" we shouted. Donald eventually lost his balance and fell. The three of us who were in on the game started to scream and shout in horror. The newbie, thinking he really fell off the roof, joined us in horror. We told the newbie "to look over to see the body" of our fallen friend. As we all screamed and sobbed uncontrollably, we pushed each other to the edge, to look over to see what happened below. One by one, we approached the edge of the roof and looked over. Each of us turned to the group with fake tears and moaning, covering our eyes, barely brave enough to view the tragedy. We signaled to the newbie to come over and look down at the horrible scene below on the street, as our flattened friend lay there like a smashed tomato. The fake waterless tears flowed, as we waved the newbie over. We thew in "Let's make up a story to tell the police, or we're all going to jail," for added torture. We bowed our heads and hid our faces as we cried uncontrollably, and repeated the lines we rehearsed.

Me and Paulie took a few steps back and held the roof newbie under the arms for strength to view the body below. "Keep your eyes open — we got you, you won't fall, keep looking down, look down." With more reassuring coaxing, the newbie got up the courage to finally and cautiously look over...only to see Donald a few feet below on the next roof, flapping his arms and feet, making "tar angels" on the roof underneath him. The crying and moaning turned to laughter as another great "GOTCHA" moment was shared by all. Now that the "roof newbie" had earned his "tar wings" in non-flight school, we could all look for another unsuspecting victim at the recruiting station, Harry's candy store. Hey, I'm just a kid...and boys will be boys, and fun is where you make it. Even at the expense of stained underwear and a few fake tears.

Mom Learns to Drive

AT THE END of the school day, the big yellow school buses were parked on the street outside PS 105 in The Bronx. These were the buses that dropped off the kids like me, who didn't live nearby and weren't walkers. The walkers had more freedom than we did. They walked back and forth from their apartments to the school, and usually made a detour into a candy store, and hung out a little before and after school. The bused-in kids left the classroom ten minutes earlier when the bell rang for early dismissal. The walkers who lived nearby stayed until three o'clock, when school was officially out. Coming home from school, the bus drove along Morris Park Avenue. As the bus approached our neighborhood, it was busier than usual. There was more traffic in the streets and there were police cars and ambulances every few blocks. On one block, there was a fire hydrant knocked over, and a high stream of water flushing out. The next block had two cars that were sideswiped, and there were police cars on the scene.

When we pulled up on my block, there were four police cars, one ambulance and a crowd of people near the corner — the same corner that was Harry's candy store and luncheonette. I hoped nothing had happened to Harry, or to his wife, Florence … since my whole life was there: I ate there, I got toys and snacks there, and played there in front of Harry's. As I got off the bus and walked toward Morris Park Avenue, toward Harry's, I saw Dad's green Rambler. The car was crashed through the Insurance and Travel Agency's storefront next to the bar. Dad's old green Rambler was smoking in the front. The front hood and fenders were smashed in, and the crumpled hood was open as the smoke poured out. The green Rambler was the car we had before Dad bought the Silver Bullet (the '57 Chevy).

The old Rambler had jumped the sidewalk and went through the plate glass window. The car was sitting on top of a six-foot model of a cruise ship that took up the whole window; above the cruise ship was a sign that read: Travel Tickets. The old man who owned the store was being taken out on a stretcher and rolled into the ambulance. In broken English, with an Italian accent, as the police followed the stretcher, he repeated over and over, "She sunka my ship, she broka everyting, she's a crazy, she's a crazy, locka her up!" He was shaking as he cried. His hands covered his face; only his nose stuck out between his hands as they rolled him into the ambulance.

Since the green Rambler was Dad's car, and Dad was at work, I knew Mom couldn't be too far away. As I got closer, someone in the crowd that gathered around the scene recognized me, I heard, "Ronnie it's your mother — she's drunk, she did this." Somehow even before that was said, I knew Mom had a hand in this. I walked through the crowd to get closer, I couldn't see her, but I could hear her. Mom was in the back seat of the police car. She wasn't just sitting there; she was yelling and kicking her feet. As she yelled and cursed, she was swinging punches wildly at the policemen on the opposite side of the car door. A few wild punches landed on the arms of the policeman who just kept pushing her back.

By now she was getting real loud — she was yelling at the policeman, "I'm just learning how to drive, what the hell you expect?"

No matter what happened, no matter what she did, Mom never apologized or was quiet when she got caught doing something wrong. She always looked at things through her drunken eyes and always had a reason for her doing wrong. So in her mind, her way of thinking was, *Hey, I told you, I'm learning to drive – how do you expect me not to have an accident?* That made sense to her. She confessed, and now she wanted out of the police car. Mom didn't see me in the crowd as they took her away in the backseat of the police car. She was too busy trying to kick her way out. If she had seen me, she'd probably have told me the same thing. It wasn't her fault.

The water from the broken fire hydrant was flooding the streets, and glass from the broken storefront was everywhere, all over the sidewalk. With the ambulance gone and the police cars gone, the small crowd broke up as the neighborhood people walked away. I walked into Harry's candy store, and sat on the red stool at the counter. I ordered an egg cream from Harry, who was behind the counter, and I asked him to make me some fries. As I drank the egg cream, I saw the tow truck hook up and tow away Dad's broken Rambler. I got off the stool and went to the window to say goodbye to the broken Rambler.

When the tow truck was out of sight I walked back to the counter and reached for an Archie comic book. I sat back down to eat my fries and sip my chocolate egg cream. This was the newest Archie comic book, so I couldn't wait to read it. The fries were hot and tasty, covered in catsup and salt, just the way I liked them. After all, I'm only seven, and I'm too young to be embarrassed.

Red Lights, Sitar Music, and Chess

SATURDAY AFTERNOONS WHEN I wasn't with my grandparents, I stayed at home at the apartment. Mom couldn't sleep all day while Dad was home, and she couldn't go to the bar either — where she went, I'll never know. Most Saturdays when Dad wasn't at the race-track he would entertain his friends, Ogden and Ronnie. Ogden was a small man, balding in the front and middle, with shoulder-length wispy hair that grew only on the sides; he looked like Bozo the Clown. He had a rough scratchy voice and always spoke very loud, almost screaming, and with every word his hands would follow. If you didn't hear his voice and just watched his gestures, you would think he was conducting an orchestra. Ronnie was also a small man; he was dark-skinned, and told everyone he was Italian and his parents came from Sicily; that's why he was so dark. He had a full head of neatly combed black hair, and he hardly ever spoke.

Ogden and Ronnie never spoke to me when they came over; I was just Buster's kid who sat in the corner. After the Saturday morning cartoons were over, Dad would set up the apartment for his arriving guests. First, he would unscrew both of the light bulbs in the table lamps, and replace them with red light bulbs. Then the console stereo would play Ravi Shankar sitar music. The chessboard would be set up on the old wood slatted coffee table that was in front of the brown couch in the living room. At the far end of the room, near the fire escape window, was where I sat at my orange desk and little wooden chair.

As soon as the boys arrived, Dad would whip out the special small, thin, stinky-smelling cigarettes that they would light up and pass around. After every puff the inhalant would choke, cough and say, "That's good shit." At seven, I didn't know you could smoke shit, and if it was so good, why would you cough and choke with every puff? After a few minutes of smoking and coughing, the choking would stop, and Dad, Ogden, and Ronnie would sit and play chess. Two would play and one would watch; the watcher played the winner when and IF the game ever ended. When the game first started, the moves were quick and there was a lot of talking among all three of them.

As all this was going on — the red lights, the sitar music — I would sit on the floor next to Dad and his opponent. Since this would happen every week, and I was an observant, quick-learning seven-year-old, I learned the game, and how every piece moved. As the game progressed, Dad, Ogden, and Ronnie would take many small, thin, stinky, choking, cigarette breaks, and they said the shit "got better and better," so they smoked more and more. By around the third game, one was on the couch snoring, and the two chess mates would nod out sleeping, waiting for the next move. Each one would wake up every few minutes, only to ask, "Who goes?"

Since I knew how to play chess, I would go. I would make the next move, black and white, playing for both sides — quietly and carefully, not to bump or wake the chess masters. The more they smoked, the more I got to play, and the less they would wake up between moves. Soon all the men would be on the couch sleeping: Dad, Ogden, and Ronnie. With everybody except me sleeping, I would turn off the music and watch TV, with hardly any sound on. After a while they would wake up and put away the chessboard, never knowing whose turn it was, who won, or that I had played the entire game, both sides.

When Dad woke up he would then shut off the TV, and put on 50s doo-wop records. Again, they would all smoke those stinky, thin cigarettes that made them cough, but now, they were all well-rested and one by one they would stand on the cocktail table and sing to the records. The one on the table sang lead; the other two did the doo-wop and were background singers. Before, every song they would introduce themselves, and it would start out: "Live from The Peppermint Lounge, it's Buster...."

Thanks to those Saturdays with Dad, Ogden and Ronnie, I know every 50s doo-wop song, and can play a good game of chess, but I never did find The Peppermint Lounge.

Square Axles Don't Bend

AN ABANDONED BABY carriage in The Bronx was not considered garbage. As Paulie and I walked through the lots, and threw rocks at our imaginary enemies, we saw an old beat-up baby carriage turned over on its side. We saw its potential, just like the caveman who marveled at a round stone and saw its potential. On our block, the older boys made street carts out of wood and carriage wheels. They would take them and ride them down the hills, down Tremont Avenue and around the block, all around the neighborhood. When on flat ground, these wooden carts had to be pushed, since they didn't have an engine. If it was your turn, you became the engine as you sat back-to-back with the pusher's legs hanging off the back. Even without an engine, when pushed, you could go pretty fast, and going down a hill, even faster as the wheels turned and carried you like a car.

We took a big stick to the old baby carriage, and managed to knock off the wheels. Now we had to find the rest of the materials to build our street-cart Cadillac. That wouldn't be hard, because the lots on Lebanon Street were like a junkyard. There really wasn't much to it; we needed three pieces of wood: one long piece for the frame, one short piece that held the front wheels in place and so we could steer it with our feet, and one shorter piece to hold the rear axle and wheels. If we wanted to be fancy, we had to find two wooden milk crates, so the driver had a seat facing forward, and the pusher had a seat facing backward, so we could sit back-to-back without leaning against each other. One kid did the steering with his feet, with a rope wrapped around the front piece of wood like the reins of a horse. It was primitive, but it worked. The other kid sat backwards and pushed with his feet dangling off the back, until we found a hill to roll down to get a free ride.

We found everything we needed in the lots on Lebanon Street. You could find anything there. It was a dumping ground for the old, the broken, or the stolen. We brought the wood, the wheels, and the axles to the front of the building — we never found the milk crates; the lots must have been out of stock. Paulie got his father's hammer and some nails. We nailed the axles to the wood by hammering the nails halfway in, then bending them over the axle until they made a complete circle over the axle, to hold it in place. Then, we hammered the other axle to the long piece of wood. With the axles in place nailed onto the wood, now we slid on the wheels, and hammered on the silver end caps we took off the baby carriage, so the wheels wouldn't fall off as they spun. The front wheels had to move to steer, so that one big nail went through both wooden pieces, and we bent the nail over so it would hold the wood in place, but it was loose enough to move right and left so we could turn and steer our street cart. At eight years old, we didn't know about nuts, bolts, and drills, since we all lived in apartments and didn't have the handiest of fathers, a tool shed, or a garage. No one fixed up or remodeled in Bronx apartments. How you moved in, was how it stayed, and that was good enough until you moved again.

Once the master builders were finished, we went out for our first push. With the excitement of the Wright brothers on their first flight, we took to the streets to glide and ride. Since I was a better salesman, I convinced Paulie to be the pusher, and I would sit and steer today, and tomorrow, we would change positions. We were so proud of our street cart — it actually worked! Paulie pushed us up the Tremont Avenue hill and we rode down real fast. As long as the ride was, and as fast as we went, we knew we had to slow down and stop before we went into the street on Morris Park Avenue. Paulie's sneaker brakes were skidding against the concrete to slow us down. It was probably

Paulie and I who invented the phrase "dragging your heels." Anyway, it worked. By the end of the day we were experienced at pushing, rolling, turning, and stopping.

After a full day of playing with our new street cart, it was getting dark. Paulie and I knew we had to hide our Cadillac, if we ever wanted to see it again. If we left it out in the open, somewhere on the street, it would not be there in the morning. Since The Bronx didn't have a lot of hiding places, we figured we would bring it back to where it was born, to the lots, to hide it. We found a great hiding spot all the way in the corner, near the last garage, behind an old burned car. We covered it up with cardboard and some big sticks and giant weeds that looked like trees, and somehow, it just blended in. When we stepped back to check it, we both smiled at our good camouflage work. We knew it blended in and would be waiting for us tomorrow morning. It was summer, so we made plans to wake up and meet early, so we could get on the road again. Paulie was more excited than me, because he was the steerer, and today I was the pusher.

On the walk home, Paulie complained how much his legs hurt and how his sneakers got beat up from pushing and stopping. The morning couldn't come fast enough. We met at Harry's candy store and ran to the lots to see if our Cadillac was still there. As we got closer, we saw nothing was disturbed; we smiled at each other like we got away with something as we removed the camouflage. It was still there, just waiting for us. Since Paulie got to steer, and I got to push, and be the brakes — for me, it wasn't as much fun as yesterday. My legs hurt from pushing and my feet burned from stopping. We were so proud of ourselves; we were doing what the big boys did, and that made us feel bigger and older since there was always a big rush to grow up. We played all day with our cart. Uphill, downhill, cruising around the block.

The same way ants know there's a picnic, a few kids from the block found us, and they all asked for ride. We wouldn't give up our cart, so we just piled them onto the cart with us to ride and push with me and Paulie. Somehow we got five of us on the cart. It wasn't comfortable, but they were our friends and we wanted to be good hosts. We rode around the block a few times laughing and screaming with delight when we would pick up speed on the turns and almost roll over. Doing dangerous things somehow makes times better. We wanted more speed and less pushing, so we decided to challenge the Tremont Avenue hill that Paulie and I had gone down yesterday. That was the hill that gave us the best ride, since it was so steep and long. We all pushed uphill while Paulie steered; it was a lot easier with five of us. When we got to the top of the hill, Paulie turned the cart around and we all piled in, on top of each other, until all five of us were somehow on the cart.

The Tremont Avenue hill lived up to its expectations; it was long and very steep. With the extra weight of three more kids, we were flying down the hill twice as fast as yesterday with just me and Paulie. We were all screaming with excitement as we rode down the hill toward the intersection of Tremont and Morris Park Avenues. This time, we couldn't slow down at the bottom of the hill. We were going too fast, and making the turn onto Morris Park Avenue wasn't possible. Paulie lost control of the cart, and my sneaker brakes didn't do such a good job of slowing us down. With the cart out of control, it hopped off the sidewalk and into the street. As the cart hit the street, with all our weight, the front axle bent, and the front wheels went flying off the axle, as we skidded into the street uncontrollably. There were oncoming cars aiming right for us, coming to a screeching halt, with car horns beeping at us as we dropped into the street with the cart out of control. Our laughter quickly turned to silence from the sudden stop; the cart rolled on top of us, as it flipped over. We were scattered in the street crying, with twisted arms and bruised legs. The people in the oncoming cars got out to help get the turned-over cart off us, out of the street, and back onto the sidewalk. Within a few minutes the traffic was moving and we were on the sidewalk, all still shook up and checking out our cuts and scrapes from what had just happened.

We looked at our broken cart. What went wrong? We were having so much fun. How could it end like this? As we stood around with teary smiles and small bruises, and tales of how fast we went, one of the older, bigger boys came out of Harry's candy store and walked toward us. He looked at us, then back at the broken cart with no wheels and said, "Square axles don't bend. If you did it right, you wouldn't be all banged up right now."

Me and Paulie looked at this kid like he was Henry Ford and Einstein rolled into one. This kid didn't invent the wheel, but he knew what kind of axles kept wheels on. His carts always worked. He didn't wind up in the middle of the street like we did. THAT'S WHY the baby carriage in the lots had been waiting there for me and Paulie. Nobody wanted it. It had round axles. It was there, while sitting on the curb, with a scraped elbow and a bloody knee, that I realized ... with age does come wisdom, and some things that are thrown out and in the lots really are garbage, and should stay there. This kid was twelve, and me, I'm only eight.

Carlo's Clubhouse

THE MAIN THING about a clubhouse is its ability to be private. Only those invited can enter. It's where close friends become closer. It's where we go to hide, to play, to be together, or just hang out. Even though playing in the streets is always fun, there's something special about a clubhouse. With a clubhouse, you don't have to include everybody, just the kids who are part of your inner circle of best friends. A clubhouse doesn't have to be elaborate.

In the winter, after a big snowstorm, on every corner in The Bronx, the plow trucks created a mountain of snow. Snow which, with a few kids, and a few shovels, became a clubhouse. We made clubhouses with the snow that the Eskimos would be proud of. We tunneled deep into the snow mound, and shoveled out a small frozen cave. This winter clubhouse would last a while, unless the weather got warmer and melted our mountain, or it was discovered and demolished by the kids who were uninvited.

When snow wasn't in season, if a new refrigerator was delivered somewhere on the block, the next day we had a new clubhouse, a big cardboard clubhouse, big enough for three or four kids. We carried the cardboard clubhouse down to the lots on Lebanon Street. We hid it, so it could last for a few days. With a broken piece of glass, we cut out two windows, so we could stand guard for kids not in the club, who wanted in. That's when the clubhouse became a fort. Sometimes if the windows weren't placed just right, you couldn't see the non-club kids, so we got stomped on while we were still inside. It was like the story of the three little pigs. Us little piggies didn't have a strong enough clubhouse, so they huffed and puffed and stomped our cardboard house down. The cardboard clubhouse never lasted long. If it rained and it got wet, the cardboard clubhouse lost its shape, and flattened out, so once again we were club-less.

On every block there was one big kid who liked playing with small kids instead of his own age group. He was a little clumsy, and slow to answer, so he was more comfortable being king of our small hill, instead of a joker on a big guy's mountain. So he stayed with the smaller kids. It worked out well. He was smarter than us, and stronger than us. He had a lot more ideas then we did. This kid was our friend Carlo. Carlo already had his membership in countless refrigerator box clubs, but he wanted a more permanent address.

Me, Carlo, and the boys searched the lots and found an abandoned car. The doors were broken and hanging, but they could be pushed in to close. The seats were ragged, and one window was smashed, but at least it wasn't wet inside. So it became our new clubhouse. After school and on weekends, we went to the Casa Del Buick, shut the doors, and hid from the non-members. There was something so cool about having a clubhouse again. The next Saturday, we met up at Harry's candy store. We walked together down the block, to the lots, to hang out in our clubhouse. Only when got there, and opened the door, a drunken homeless man rolled out. We ran. I guess we were even — we scared him, and he scared us. We went back later, and he was still in our clubhouse, and he wasn't even a member.

The next day, we met up and went back to the clubhouse. We quietly snuck up on the old Buick and looked inside; the drunk home-less guy was sleeping in the back seat, with his shoes and socks off. He left his shoes and socks outside the door of the car, like it was an apartment, and he didn't want to get it dirty. He was a full-grown man, and he looked scary when he was awake, so we let him sleep. Now, it was official: this was his new home, no longer our clubhouse. That day we looked for another abandoned car or even a refrigerator box to relocate the club, but nothing. We had no clubhouse. Nothing to call our own. Nothing to hang out in. As we walked through the lots club-less and searching, Carlo pointed to the train tracks above us, about twenty-five feet high. As he pointed, he said, "There's our new club-house — it's real secret; no one would ever find us, and it's always dry."

The only problem was that we had to climb a steel brace trestle to get up there. Carlo went first since it was his idea. He was like Columbus, discovering the new world. He climbed cautiously up the metal rafters, and actually got up there. Even though it was high up, it wasn't a steep climb. He had to go up hand over hand. It was like climbing large monkey bars on the school playground, only bigger. He climbed until he was surrounded by concrete and steel beams, with the train tracks above his head.

"Find some wood," Carlo said. "I'll lay it across the beams to make a floor." When the new president of the club (since he found it) gave a command, we listened. We all ran around searching for wood. There were three of us on the ground — me, Donald, and Paulie. We each came back with plenty of scrap pieces of wood. The lots never let us down. It was a dumping ground for everything, and if you looked hard enough, you could find anything. It was a scavenger hunt, and we were the scavengers. Donald stayed on the ground and handed the pieces up to Paulie, who handed them up to me, and I handed them up to Carlo. We looked like little worker ants who were making their nest.

Carlo laid the long pieces of wood across the beams and made a floor, sort of. We climbed back down and looked for more unburied treasure. We found old chairs, and boxes for tables, and an old mat-tress that we dragged up to the sky-high club. After everything was put in its place, we dropped the mattress over the wood floor and lay on it for the rest of the afternoon, thinking, *How cool is this club-house? This is the Fort Knox of clubhouses.* We were surrounded by steel and concrete. No big bad uninvited wolf could blow this down.

We lay there until it started to get dark and we all had to go home. We climbed down slow and careful, holding on tight, so as not to fall. Climbing down things is harder than climbing up things, since feet don't have eyes and a brain. Before we could let one hand go, our foot was placed on the iron bar underneath, as we climbed down stretching to reach the rung below, like a giants' ladder.

After school, we met up at the club. We brought up soda and candy. To defend our clubhouse, we made rubber band guns that shot pieces of cut-up linoleum instead of bullets. We called them "carpet guns." Each piece was cut into a little square, about an inch. We put the little squares into the rubber band, and then pulled it back. The rubber band was held in place by a clothespin, secured by more rubber bands so it held in place, like a trigger. Rubber bands are like kids' nails when you don't have a hammer! It worked like a slingshot, only not as accurate. These weapons could be used in case we were discovered, and had to defend our clubhouse. We could shoot down at the enemy, as our clubhouse turned into our fort. Every day we went to the clubhouse, and we kept it a secret from the kids on the block. This was truly a perfect clubhouse; all we needed was running water and electricity. Instead, we suffered with Cokes and flashlights.

Our perfect clubhouse didn't last long, though. One afternoon, after being in the clubhouse all day, it was getting dark. We had to climb down to go home. Since he was older and the official club leader, Carlo was always the first to climb up, and the first to climb down. We knew the danger of the climb, so we watched Carlo as he placed his feet and hands strategically from one girder to the lower one below. Around the neighborhood, Carlo was not known for his cat-like moves. He was considered clumsy. Being clumsy twenty-five feet up in the air, holding on to a steel girder ... this is not a desirable quality. His foot felt around for the steel step below, but before his hand secured the next beam, in the time it takes to wink an eye, he slipped, and fell from the steel girders. As he fell, his body hit the steel brace that crossed through the girders that held it in place. It was shaped like a big "X" to secure the beams to the concrete. When Carlo hit the ground below, he wasn't moving. He was knocked out. He looked like he was dead or asleep. I looked in horror as he lay there motionless.

Seeing him on the ground made us scarred to climb down, but we had to. We had to get to Carlo, and get help. My hands and feet climbed down the steel beams more carefully than ever before. My hands were sweaty, and my legs shook like there was an earthquake. Somehow I made it to the ground without falling. Paulie was right behind me, climbing down making noises like he couldn't breathe. We looked at Carlo; he still wasn't moving. Donald was making his way down real slow. When he was a few feet from the ground, he jumped. He looked at Carlo, and froze, and put his hands on his head, like we were playing Simon Says.

Me and Paulie ran up the street to Harry's candy store and told Harry and Florence what happened. Harry came around the counter; he walked as fast as he could with his bad leg to the phone booth, and called the police. The police called an ambulance. We ran back to the lots to Carlo. He was still on the ground, but now awake and screaming in pain. He said, "I can't move — get my mother, get my mother." We stayed with Carlo till the ambulance came. The three of us watched as Carlo, unable to move, remained on his back, crying.

When you're anxious, time moves like molasses in the winter. It felt like a very long time before the police and ambulance came. Carlo was one of the big, strong guys on the block. If he was this hurt, us smaller kids wouldn't stand a chance after a fall like that. As the ambulance came, two men swung open the back doors and lifted Carlo on a stretcher. They pushed him inside the already open doors in the back of the ambulance, then slammed them shut. One stayed in the back with Carlo. The other got in the driver's seat. The ambulance sped away; the siren filled our ears, and the tires shot pebbles as the ambulance left the lots. We weren't sure what was to become of Carlo. How seriously was he hurt? Would he be okay? We ran to get Carlo's mother and tell her what happened, and about his being taken away in an ambulance to the hospital. How could we do this, without getting all of us in trouble? We could say that we were just playing in the lots and Carlo got hurt. After all, our clubhouse was dangerous, and telling the truth didn't sound like a good idea. What happened to

Carlo could have happened to any one of us. Our quest to find and build a great clubhouse turned out awful!

We ran to Carlo's house to tell his mother, Irene. We knocked on the door and rang the bell, but no one answered. We stayed on the stoop of the three-story house and continued to knock, and ring the doorbell. After a few minutes of nobody answering, we ran back to Harry's candy store to see who knew what happened, and where could we find Carlo's mom to tell her. If I couldn't find Irene, I knew where I could find her sister Eleanor. She and my mother drank at the bar in the afternoon before their husbands came home.

I ran into the bar to tell Eleanor what happened. I saw Mom and Eleanor and could hardly get the words out of my mouth. My breathing was fast and I was nervous. I spoke loud so they could hear me over the music that was playing. They looked at me as I told them what happened to Carlo. Without saying a word, as she shared at me. Eleanor picked up her glass, and drank her drink down in one gulp. She shouted,"Somebody drive me to the hospital." She looked at my mother and said,"Candy, come with me." Eleanor, and all adults on the block, called my mother Candy. They took their pocketbooks, and left their lit cigarettes in the ashtray, then left the bar together. One of the neighborhood guys drove them in a light-blue Cadillac with a white top. They burned rubber as they went down Morris Park Avenue.

Everything was happening so fast .My mother left with Eleanor, as I stood there uncomfortably in the bar. I walked out of the bar, and the kids in the neighborhood came up to me and asked me what happened. I didn't answer any of them. I went into Harry's, and sat on the chrome stool with a red leather seat at the counter. I pretended nothing was wrong. I asked Harry for a cherry Coke. Harry looked at me from the corner of his eye, as he squirted the cherry into the Coke, and poured seltzer in the glass. He stirred it with a long silver spoon and said, "If you kids stayed out of the lots, this wouldn't have happened."

Harry's voice was more stern than usual, but he was right. I saw what could, and did happen. Harry never said much, but when he spoke to you, you listened. He didn't soften his delivery when he spoke, even though I'm just a kid. His cold blue eyes stared at me without blinking. I could feel the seriousness of what happened. I didn't answer Harry back or talk to him. He wasn't the kind of man a kid should test. I thought to myself, *How could something that started out so great change so quickly?* Maybe what made our clubhouse so great was the added element of danger, as we climbed the iron girders twenty-five feet high to get there. That, and it was hidden and not accessible to outsiders. That's what made our clubhouse so special, at least until Carlo got hurt.

Donald left the candy store and went home. Me and Paulie sat at the counter at Harry's. All we could talk about was Carlo on the stretcher and the ambulance that took him away to the hospital. Even though I was sorry for Carlo, I was glad it wasn't me who fell. I felt awful for feeling that way, but it was true. Play time and safety don't go hand-in-hand when you're a kid playing in the streets.

Carlo was in the hospital for almost a month. We didn't see him until he came home. When he first came home, his mother let us in the house to see him whenever we came over. After a while, when we knocked on the door, she stopped letting us in. I didn't like it, but I understood why. In some way she held us responsible for what happened to Carlo. She saw us walking around and our lives were the same, and Carlo was in bed with a body cast. She was angry, because even though it could have happened to any one of us, it was her son who got hurt. After school and on weekends, we continued to play in the lots, but we never climbed back up to the clubhouse. That was the last of the clubhouses. Seeing what happened to Carlo made us scared...and being scared takes the fun out of everything.

The Bronx Zoo

WHERE I LIVED on Tremont and Morris Park Avenue, if you walked down Tremont Avenue into West Farms area, you could get to the rear entrance of The Bronx Zoo. If you walked along the fence long enough, eventually there would be an opening where someone snipped out a section of fence big enough to climb through. At seven years old, I didn't know it was stealing; we called it getting in for free. The only person old enough and bold enough to go to the zoo without an adult or parent was Stewie. Stewie was my uncle; he was only two years older than me. My mom got pregnant and had me at eighteen years old, and my grandmother had Uncle Stewie when she was forty. He was my mom's baby brother. We were so close in age that when we would declare, "That's my uncle," or "He's my nephew," no one believed us. It was always our source of amusement to tell people how we were related.

Stewie lived in The Bronx River projects with his parents, my grandparents, and he was a great traveler. He loved to walk and knew every shortcut, no matter how dangerous. To get to see me, he walked through two abandoned lots, over a dozen streets, and ran across two highways — The Bronx River Highway and the Tremont overpass. Parents — at least, our parents — didn't know or care what we did during the day; supervision in The Bronx in the '60s was not high on the priority list for parents. Parents in my neighborhood had no structured activities; anything was okay as long as we came home after it got dark.

That afternoon, Stewie got to the apartment about noon, and he had a bag of sandwiches he made for us. I contributed a bottle of soda, and snowball cakes from Bernie's grocery store downstairs. One pink, one white, they were the sweetest cupcakes in the world. There was so much sugar in those cupcakes. After a few bites, you got an instant cavity check. The sugar found a hole in your tooth and you had to open your mouth to let in air to calm down the cavity.

When Stewie and I would go to the zoo, we mostly would walk, but sometimes to make me laugh, he would say, "Let's run!" I was an average runner, but Stewie was more athletic and incredibly strong for his age and size, and when he ran, he could easily lose me. So as he would look at me and say,"Let's run." He would then grab my hand and run, actually pulling me so fast that my feet would barely touch the ground. He nearly lifted me off the pavement. The faster he ran and the harder he pulled me, the more I laughed and the slower I ran, so once we started to crack up laughing, he would trot down to a walk, then walk the rest of the way.

Once inside the zoo, we never missed the feeding of the lions and tigers. The big cathouse, as we called it, fed the lions at 3:30. The lions and tigers were in cages, and it was indoors and looked like a big cement prison. As soon as you entered the building, you were overcome with a deep gamy smell. It was a combination of the animal scent and urine. The growls and snarls of the lions and tigers were at such a low frequency that when they bellowed, you could feel the vibration in your body, like you were sitting on a bass speaker from a stereo system. Even though they were behind bars, their size and growl made me not get close to the cages. Not Stewie — he was fearless. He would climb the railing in front of each cage and touch the metal bars on the cages that separated us from the lions. The big cats would pace back and forth and bellow their deep growls and my arm hair would stand up and give me goose bumps.

After the lion house, we went to the monkey house. The monkeys were active; they played and swung on ropes and branches. They didn't look unhappy like the lions and tigers; the monkeys looked like they didn't mind being there, or at least they had each other, and were making the best of it. They were held in groups and were more social animals. I liked the long hair, and color of the orangutans. They looked orange and tan, and that's how I thought they got their name … orange-u-tan. I also liked the monkey house because before we left, I could make fun of Stewie's ears and get away with it; his ears were big, and stuck out like a monkey's, but it was funny only in the monkey house … poor monkeys, for having Stewie's ears.

After walking through The Bronx Zoo and seeing the animals, we would sit and eat our sandwiches on the grass, and drink the sodas and eat the cavity- finding cakes: the snowballs, white for me, pink for Stewie. Those were special days, and I knew to appreciate them. I never wanted them to end. Me, Stewie, and The Bronx Zoo. How lucky I am at seven to have all this.

Outrunning Bobo

THE NAME BOBO was usually followed by "He's going to get you." Everyone on the block was frightened to death, afraid of Bobo. Bobo was a very, very big tan dog that never stopped barking and showing his teeth. He growled and chomped down on the air with every breath, as if he was biting down on an arm or leg. Bobo was the building superintendent's dog. Bobo lived outside the super's apartment entrance; he was on a long chain and a choke collar with spikes that tightened around his neck as he pulled the chain to its length's end. His eyes were black and lifeless, and he never blinked. If you walked anywhere near Bobo's area, he went crazy; he tried his best to get you, barking, pulling and showing his teeth with a growl that translated in human language to "stay away."

Kids being kids and always seeking mischievous adventure, we often went to test Bobo and the strength of this chain. When Bobo saw us and charged to get us, as long as we calculated the length of this chain, we knew we could taunt him at a safe distance. We knew it was wrong, but what else could you do with Bobo? You couldn't play with him. You couldn't make him fetch. You couldn't bring him a bone. You couldn't pet him. To the young boys on the block, it was almost a rite of passage, a way to challenge your courage, by facing Bobo. To test your manhood, as Bobo with all his ferocity tried to break the chains that bound him to get you and rip you apart.... It was perhaps the same way the young boys in Spain would pretend to be bullfighters by standing before a cow or young bull, stepping forward with a red cape to test their courage and the animal's weakness. The difference was that we saw no weakness in Bobo; he never stopped moving forward, even as a spiked collar tightened and choked his thick, muscular neck. That chain was the only thing that kept us safe as he barked and growled and showed his teeth. We never lost our fear of Bobo. It was there. At eight years old I realized that fear brings respect, and respect creates boundaries, and ours was twenty feet of chain ... not courage.

Cinque Bets

IN THE SUMMER when I was off from school and slept over at Nanny's house, twice a week we went to visit her mother, my great-grandma, Grandma Pavone. On those days, we had to get up early and take the train to 138th Street in Harlem. That's where Grandma Pavone lived. Nanny, her brothers and sister, grew up in that apartment. Nanny told me she was just a little girl when she and her family left Italy to come to America. The Pavone family was her father Peter, mother Columbia, older brother Concepcion (they called him Jim), Brother Eddie, and her baby sister Marion. Nanny was the eldest girl. That meant she was the one who would help her mother raise the family. From an early age, Nanny learned to cook and clean the house and shop for groceries. Nanny was a real-life Cinderella. She put her family's needs above her own, and it remained that way.

Her father, Peter, was a carpenter in Italy. When he reached America, he had difficulty finding work. Even though they moved to an Italian neighborhood, where mostly everyone spoke Italian, once off their street, America was a foreign country to them, since only her brothers and sister learned to speak English. Great-grandpa Peter spent his days sitting at the window watching the streets below. He sat on an old wooden chair with a faded red leather seat. His elbows rested on his bed pillow, to cushion his thin, frail arms, as he watched the world outside. His face drooped from age, and he had no teeth to align his face. When he spoke, his voice was soft, and sounded like he was singing … it was almost musical. It sounded like the little mandolin Uncle Eddie played, which was hidden under his bed, and taken out only on special occasions. Since I didn't speak Italian and he didn't speak English, I knew what he said by his hand gestures. As soon as I came into the apartment, he waved me over, gently rubbed my head, and held my chin as he kissed both of my cheeks. The aroma of wine remained on my cheeks all day after he kissed me hello. There was a big jug of red wine by his ankles that he sipped while looking out the window.

The train ride there wasn't so long, but the climb up the steps to the platform of the train station was like climbing a mountain in the summer's heat. Even though our hands were wet with perspiration, Nanny never let go of my hand, except when we had to separate to go through the turnstile, after we put in our train tokens. The highlight of the train ride was the pennies Nanny gave me, which I put in the gum machine in the middle of the platform while we waited for the train.

Grandma Pavone lived on the fourth floor. After walking upstairs, Nanny pushed open the door that was never locked, and within minutes, after she kissed her mother, she started to do laundry by hand in a washtub, as her mother watched. She scrubbed the dirty clothes on something that looked like a big cheese grater. Grandma Pavone was a short, gray-haired woman who lacked vanity. Her hair was never combed, and she wore no makeup. A giant wrinkled apron always covered her dress. She wore Great-grandpa's leather slippers, with her stockings rolled down to her ankles. As Nanny washed and hung out the laundry to dry on the clothesline, I handed her the clothespins that were kept by the window in a cloth bag. Before I handed them to Nanny, to make her laugh, I put a clothespin on my nose, like I saw Moe do to Curly, on *The Three Stooges*. When finished, Nanny and Grandma Pavone made out a shopping list so she could shop for her mother, the way she had since she was a child. Grandma Pavone didn't speak English, and never left the house; if she had, she would've learned that Italian wasn't spoken in her neighborhood anymore. Most people her age had passed away, or moved long ago.

Grandma Pavone never spoke to me, not even with Nanny as the interpreter. To her, I was just the kid Nanny dragged around a few days a week, when she came to see her. She never offered me any- thing, no food, no drink, nothing ... ever. She acted like she was mad at me for some reason. She lacked the warmth you would expect from an old person — especially since we were related. Most older people show kindness toward children, but not her. I asked Nanny about that. I asked her why Grandma wasn't a nice or happy person. She told me her mother didn't like America. She left her homeland and all of her family back in Italy to come to America for a better life. She never learned the new language or made friends, and she was always suspicious of others.

Nanny told me the story of when they first came to America. They came with wooden crates that her father made back in Italy for the voyage to America. In the crates were clothing, silverware, and fine linens and bed sheets. On the sheets, pillowcases, and towels there were her mother's initials, C.P. (Columbia Pavone), stitched in bold fancy lettering. They were given to her mother as wedding presents by her family, and she cherished them. As they moved into the apart- ment, the same apartment where they still lived, the trunks were stolen on the front steps of the building. She told me that soon after, Grandma Pavone saw her sheets hanging off her neighbor's clothes- line. There was no doubt they were hers, since they had her initials. She told her husband what she saw, and she knew who had stolen her sheets. Great-grandpa Peter confronted the family that had the sheets; he was told they were a present from some very big people in the neighborhood, and not to make trouble. He was told, "Buy new sheets if you know what's good for you, pretend you didn't see what you saw." Welcome to America. They left Italy, only to live with cor- rupt Italians in the American slums of Harlem.

With work as a carpenter scarce and having to provide for four children, times were tough for the Pavones. Then tragedy struck the family when the eldest son, Concepcion (Jim) died at sixteen years old from pneumonia, because they couldn't afford medical care. Now I understood why Grandma Pavone was never happy. Her dreams died with poverty, and corruption, and her child. Me and Nanny walked fast to complete our list, almost running from grocer to butcher to baker, to finish the food shopping. She wanted to be back in time for Granddad. This meant we had to finish the shopping, put it away, and catch the train back to Crosby Avenue in time to have dinner on the table for Granddad by five o'clock when he came home from work.

As we placed the bags on the table, and took out the items one by one, Grandma Pavone began yelling at Nanny in Italian. I didn't understand what they were saying, but I knew by her tone, it wasn't good. Nanny never raised her voice as her mother shouted at her. She answered back in a soft voice, "But Mama, cinque bets, cinque bets." Then she opened her change purse and emptied it on the kitchen table. Grandma Pavone continued to shout in Italian, but now her arms moved like a windmill, as her voice got louder. Nanny walked to the window where her father sat. She kissed his hands, his cheeks, and his forehead, as I waved goodbye from the kitchen. Grandma Pavone slammed the door behind us. You could still hear Grandma Pavone yelling, "Cinque bets, cinque bets," until we were on the second floor staircase. Only the distance between us silenced her. I knew she was still yelling "Cinque bets" until the train reached Crosby Avenue.

On the train ride home, I asked, "Nanny, what is cinque bets, and why does Grandma Pavone keep yelling it?"

She told me," Cinque bets is five dollars, and Grandma thinks I should have given her more change back, because what I bought could not have cost five dollars."

I asked her, "Does she think you didn't do a good shopping, or you took her money?"

Nanny said, "It costs ten dollars or more every week to shop, so I have her five dollars and I put in my five dollars, then I give her whatever change I have left in my purse to keep her quiet, but it never works; this goes on every week."

I said, "Nanny, if you have to do the laundry, and shop, and take trains, and get yelled at, why do you go?"

Nanny looked into my eyes, and with a deep breath and a sigh, she said, "That's my mother."

Nothing more needed to be said. Somehow I understood what she meant. I put my head on Nanny's chubby pillow of an arm, and leaned my shoulder against hers, as I counted down the train stops to Crosby Avenue. The movement of the train rocked us back and forth between stops. Nanny closed her eyes and puffed a few times as she napped. We had to hurry home, back to the apartment, so Nanny could cook for Granddad before he came home from work. As I watched Tom and Jerry cartoons in the living room while Nanny cooked, it came to me that no matter how Grandma Pavone yelled at Nanny, she would be back again in a few days to take care of her. Nanny's love and devotion to her mother was worth more than cinque bets.

Aunt Marion

THE SAME WAY Nanny went to her mother's house to shop and clean, she also went to her baby sister's, Marion. Aunt Marion lived near Park Chester, on Castle Hill Avenue. We had to take two buses to see her. First we rode the number twenty-eight bus to Westchester Square, then the number four bus that rode along Tremont Avenue. Just like when we visited her mother, Grandma Pavone, we had to be back early, so Nanny could cook for Granddad by five o'clock. She wanted dinner on the table so he couldn't get mad at her for visiting her sister.

Aunt Marion was ten years younger than Nanny, but to look at her, it didn't seem so. She was heavy, and sickly with emphysema. If she laughed too hard, or too long, she quickly ran out of air, and was gasping for breath, holding her chest. She had such a hard time breathing that she couldn't go food shopping for herself, or do much cleaning around the apartment. Unlike visiting Grandma Pavone, Aunt Marion came to life when we would visit. She and Nanny would embrace and kiss each other, like it had been too long, even though they saw each other just a few days ago. The way they held each other, to them, their separation felt much longer. They held each other and turned in a circle, like two dancing bears at a Russian circus. Then, like all visits, they began to whisper and laugh, until Aunt Marion's face got as red as a tomato when she couldn't catch her breath. They had a genuine love for each other that only two sisters could share. I never saw Granddad greet his brothers like that, even though they loved each other. When Aunt Marion called her sister, she called her "Millie." She sang her name in a high-pitched voice in two syllables, "Mill-Lee," and her name sounded like an opera. Every time she called Nanny "Millie," it sounded like she was calling somebody else — to me she was "Nanny."

Unlike their mother, when Nanny went to shop, Aunt Marion reached in her pocketbook and handed Nanny her wallet, with trust and appreciation for her help. Before Nanny shopped, they cleaned the apartment together. Aunt Marion tried to help Nanny clean, but after a few minutes she was out of breath. Nanny went to her and rubbed her shoulders. In a sympathetic voice she said, "Go into the kitchen, make yourself some hot tea, and sit for a while."

After the apartment was clean, Nanny got ready to go shopping. Aunt Marion loved having company, so before Nanny could get her purse to leave, she said, "Leave little Ronnie with me." She, like her sister, was very giving and affectionate. As soon as the door closed behind Nanny, she gave me soda and cookies and I watched television, as Aunt Marion sat at the kitchen table and drank hot tea with a shot of whiskey in it. As she poured the whiskey, she said, "Don't tell Nanny about this, it will be our little secret."

When Nanny got back from shopping, they both put away the groceries as Nanny handed back Aunt Marion's wallet. She never checked her receipts or the money left in her wallet, like their mother did. They worked like a team together; Nanny took the groceries out of the shopping bags and Aunt Marion put everything away. When I wasn't supposed to know something, they spoke in Italian, and laughed together, like there was a comedian in the room.

Aunt Marion lived on the second floor and when her husband, Uncle Georgie, was working, she spent her days looking out of her window at the world below. If she was well enough and could climb the stairs, I'm sure she'd be sitting with the women in front of the building on folding beach chairs. She saw us coming down the street before we saw her, since she had a bird's-eye view. By the time we walked up the stairs to her apartment, before we could knock, the door automatically opened, with Aunt Marion standing there with a happy face on.

Her apartment was small, and even though the furniture was old, everything was in its place. It was what Nanny called "tidy." In the middle of Aunt Marion's living room was a huge black-and-white console television. It had more cabinet than television. Alongside it, there were metal folding snack trays filled with candy, in the same glass candy bowl that Nanny had. On the other table, there was a stack of *TV Guides*, with famous television people smiling on the covers. It must be a law not to frown if you're on television. Aunt Marion never got visitors, so she looked forward to Nanny's visits, since she didn't get out much. Even though she lived on the second floor, climbing up and down the few steps of the building were difficult for her. She said she wished she had an elevator in her building, followed by "Uncle Georgie didn't make enough money to move to a better neighborhood with a new building that has an elevator." So, she remained a prisoner in the apartment, even though it was only a few steps to freedom. Going outside was an occasion she looked forward to.

Aunt Marion was a big woman; she was taller and wider than Nanny. She had dyed red hair that was cut short and very curly, with a texture like the Brillo pad she kept under the sink. A handful of bobby pins held her curly sideburns in place, in front of her ears. She wore red lipstick that extended over her lips, to make her thin lips look larger than they really were. She had my Nanny's nose, which was a little too big for feminine faces. Like Nanny, she had no eyebrows; they were drawn on in brown pencil, a little higher from where they should have been, so it made her eyes look bigger than they were, and she looked surprised all the time. She had beauty marks on her face, and one near her lips that she darkened to make it stand out like Marilyn Monroe's.

When Nanny went to the store, Aunt Marion went to the window to sneak a cigarette while I watched television. I pretended not to see her, but I did, and with the summer's breeze, the smoke blew back into the apartment and filled the air. After the cigarette, she chewed spearmint gum to hide the smell of the cigarettes on her breath before Nanny got back from the store. With her emphysema, and trouble breathing, she wasn't supposed to smoke, but she did anyway.

Aunt Marion and Uncle Georgie had a son named Peter, who, like his father, was a printer. He worked with his father every day, and on their days off, they went fishing together. On their way to work, they made sure to pick each other up for the long ride. They had lunch together and worked the printing presses together. When his father spoke, Peter had a big grin on his face, as if he was waiting for a punch line of a joke. Uncle Georgie wasn't a funny guy; it was just that Peter truly loved his father and listened with a smile of approval to his words. Granddad said that Uncle Georgie was a drunk, but I never saw him drink. I knew what a drunk acted like, and smelled like and spoke like, since my mother was one.

Like all the women in my family, Aunt Marion didn't work; she filled her days at her window sneaking puffs from Uncle Georgie's cigarettes, which she stole from his pocket the night before. She sat at the window and waited for "the boys" — that's what she called them — to come home. She had no friends, just family, but didn't seem to mind. She waited for Uncle Georgie's day off. On that day they got up early, and drove the old blue Ford Galaxy with no muffler to Montauk. They drove one hundred miles just to get out, take a drive, and share a hot dog from a truck stop on the side of the road. She told Nanny that was their entertainment, and she liked the change of scenery.

It was now about four o'clock, and Nanny and I had to leave Aunt Marion's to get home in time to make Granddad's dinner. Nanny and Aunt Marion enjoyed being with each other for the day, and both were sad to see the day end, even though they would speak to each other tonight on the phone in just a few hours after dinner. They hugged and kissed each other like it was their last goodbye, even though they would see each other in just a few days. That's how strong their love was for each other. Aunt Marion hugged and kissed me the same way. She squeezed me like a wrestler, so hard I thought she snapped my spine. She gave me a dollar that she pressed into my palm. It was folded down to the size of a matchbook, and she said, "Get some candy later; don't tell Nanny," as she winked one eye at me, like it was a secret.

Nanny saw everything, and smiled her approval. That's the way they were: two sisters, one heart...one mind...one love.

Granddad's Room

IN MY GRANDDAD'S room where I slept, there was a small white desk with black legs. On top of the desk was a picture scrapbook. It was held together with rubber bands and bakery box string, the red and white kind you got when you bought a cake from the bakery on Crosby Avenue. The binding was broken, and cellophane tape held some of the pictures in place. The rest of the pictures were loose and out of any order. Something about the picture album didn't seem right. It contained pictures of only my grandfather's life, as if his life were separate from his family. There were no pictures of our family. No pictures of his children, no pictures of his wife, no pictures of his grandchildren, no pictures of his eight brothers and three sisters or their children. The photos were of his life and the things he was.

There were plentiful pictures of his military career. One picture was when he was an Army private in Fort Dix, New Jersey. In this picture he was very young, his hair was dark black and he was very skinny. He had a cigarette in one hand, and he was standing on one leg, laughing. I never knew Granddad smoked. To see him young looked strange to me. I never knew him then. I just know him now, at this age. I pulled this one out and showed it to Granddad. I asked him why he was standing on one leg, laughing. He told me this was how he would look if he got his leg blown off in the war. I asked him, "What war? What war were you in?" He said, "All three." Wow! My granddad was in three wars, so I guess he was lucky not to have his leg blown off.

I went into the kitchen and I asked Nanny about the picture; she told me he was never in the Army, or any wars. She said he was in the National Guard and he never left New Jersey. Now I was confused — Granddad was in three wars, but in New Jersey? I saw John Wayne war movies on television, and the wars were always fought in another country. Not New Jersey. I knew New Jersey was here in America, and close to The Bronx. Granddad had a sister that lived in New Jersey, and we went to visit her. I didn't think any wars were ever fought in New Jersey. Maybe Granddad was in so many wars that he was confused, too.

Even though Granddad was a private in the Army, he borrowed a sergeant's uniform, and took pictures as a sergeant. He also had pictures of himself with a long red-tailed coat with a black bonnet with a feather on it. I think it was really a marching band outfit. Granddad thought it was a general's parade uniform. One Saturday he dressed up in this uniform. Then we walked into the living room and he draped an American flag behind him. He gave me his camera and told me to take his picture. The flag was thumb tacked over the old wooden blinds in the living room window so it hid the street outside. He wanted to make the picture look like it was taken on a military base.

Some pictures were of him saluting with the helmet on. Other pictures were when he was standing at what he called "at ease." When I asked him what "at ease" meant, he said, "It's when you're not standing at attention." Granddad sure knew a lot of military words, but that word I remembered. In school when all the kids went into the auditorium, the principal would tell us to stand at attention. So we all stood up straight and stiff like soldiers, like Granddad. Then he had me take his picture with the helmet in his left hand, and with his right hand he was saluting the flag. Even though I'm just a kid, I must have taken good pictures because all the pictures I took were in his picture box.

As I dug deeper into Granddad's Tom McCann shoebox under the picture album, I found pictures of him being a cowboy, with rodeo pictures taken at the L.B. Ranch (those were his initials). I never knew he had a ranch. I knew Granddad had a bad back, so he couldn't ride those horses. None of the pictures were action pictures with the horses moving underneath him; he posed for them. He was sitting on top of these horses holding the reins and flashing his movie star rehearsed smile. As I flipped one photo over, it read "Lee's horse Torch." That was the only cowboy photo with a name of a horse he sat on, so it must have been his favorite.

I looked through more of Granddad's pictures. Now I saw pictures of his music career. There were pictures of him holding a small stick in his right hand, leading an orchestra. It was the same kind of stick my music teacher held when she directed us on when to sing in the glee club. In Granddad's handwriting on the back of the picture it said: "The Len Lavere Orchestra." There were other pictures of him, this time sitting behind a full set of drums. On the back they all read "Len Lavere." I never knew his other name was Len Lavere. He also had pictures of his brothers, and a trio they had. They were called "The Three Brothers." Now that made sense; there were three of them, and they were really brothers. There were pictures of his brothers Paulie and Scotty. They all wore white suits with white shirts and black silk ties. They all looked like movie stars and had the same movie star smile as they looked into the camera.

Then I found more pictures of Granddad in his solo career. He cut out names of popular clubs and hotels and pasted them on this blackboard and put his photo in the middle, so you would think he played at these places. Then Granddad had full pages of newspaper prints taped together to make a few sentences about his act. Under his picture was "Lee Wows 'em." The size and shapes of the words were all different, so even I knew it was not really from the same newspaper. Those words were never meant to be together. It was put together like a ransom note. I guess Granddad thought he was fooling the people who came to see him play his guitar and sing.

Then there were pictures with Granddad's head cut out and taped onto someone else's body. It was easy to spot this, since Granddad's head was either too big or too small to fit on that guy's body, unless he was a cartoon character. On the back of one picture it read "Lee and Frank Sinatra." That name I knew, since Granddad played his records. I went back into the kitchen to ask Nanny about Granddad playing music with Frank Sinatra. She told me they were on the same stage, but not at the same time. Granddad played that club twenty years after Sinatra did. I showed her the pictures of Granddad's head taped over photos, so it looked like he was there. She shook her head back and forth and made a sound with her mouth, clicking her tongue to her teeth, and all she said was "Your grandfather!"

As I looked through the pictures and all the things he had on the wall, I was confused. Most people, when you meet them, tell you what they are. Some people are teachers. Some people are bus drivers. Some people are carpenters. But what did Granddad tell people he was? Was he all of these things? To listen to him at dinner time, when he told stories about being in the Army, and being a musician, and being a cowboy, I think he thought he was all of these things. Why not? Even though I'm just a kid, so far I was a fireman, I was a policeman, and a baseball player, and now I wanted to own a candy store. So why couldn't Granddad be all these things that were in his room? Someday, when I would be old like Granddad, maybe I'd have a room like his, and when you looked around, and you saw all the things I was, you would say, "He's just like his granddad."

Me, Paulie, and the Ventures

BEFORE THERE WAS air guitar, there was cardboard guitar. I know, because I invented it with my friend Paulie. When it rained outside or there were not enough kids to play with, we would go to his second-floor walkup apartment. His apartment was always dark and very warm; you could hear the steam radiator in the corner hissing away, and the windows covered in moisture from the cold air outside. Paulie's parents worked, and we were always home alone. We heard "Pipeline" by the Ventures in Harry's candy store during the week on the Wurlitzer jukebox as we sat and had lime rickey sodas.

On Saturday we walked to Park Chester to the record store, and for 99 cents we bought "Pipeline" by the Ventures on a "45" size record. The entire time we walked, we fantasized about playing Pipeline, and we made guitar sounds with our mouths. We walked back to Paulie's house and put "Pipeline" on his parents' hi-fi, and we listened to "Pipeline" over and over and over. We motioned with our left hands the fingering of the notes, and with our right hands the strumming of the strings. The next day we found a refrigerator box, and with chalk and scissors, we cut out the first cardboard guitar. The first guitar didn't come out too good, but the second one had a longer neck and a better shape to it. Somehow I convinced Paulie that he should take the first guitar and I should take the second guitar. We brought our cardboard guitars up to Paulie's apartment and began to play along with the Ventures. This was going along great all week — me, Paulie, and the Ventures — until something happened.

Paulie was curious; he liked the Ventures song "Pipeline" so much that he wanted to see what was on the flip side of the record. It was "Wipeout." "Wipeout" was all drums, all the time. Some guitar, but it featured the drums. Paulie's face lit up. Now I knew I had lost Paulie. Paulie wanted to be a drummer now. He got his mother's long wooden spoons she stirred sauce with and used the leather footstool like a drum. He played along to "Wipeout," and I fingered the cardboard guitar. We were a great act — the longer we played, the more we were convinced we were real musicians. Paulie wanted "Wipeout," since he played the drums; I wanted "Pipeline" so I could play the cardboard guitar. Our musical preferences started to show — we disagreed on what side to play, and so, we decided to break up the band. We still were good friends and played together in the street, but our musical brotherhood was finished. I guess our artistic differences separated us, even at our tender age of seven.

I Know It's Mine

MY GRANDDAD AND his family were all musicians of some sort. He came from a big family. He had eight brothers and three sisters. Some became professional musicians, and some were good enough to play only at family house parties and get-togethers. When I was with Granddad, I watched him play guitar. When he took a break and left the room, I would pick it up and play it. I had to memorize how he left it, and put it back in the exact same way on the couch, so he didn't know I'd touched it. The brown tortoiseshell pick was placed between the strings in the middle of the guitar neck. The soft piece of red velvet that covered the strings when it was in the case was crumpled near where the guitar neck and body became one. It was so big and impressive-looking. Granddad called it a blonde, because the color of the grained wood was the color of blonde hair. Even though my fingers weren't long or thick like Granddad's, I was able to play Granddad's guitar. I also figured out a few songs by ear and fingered and strummed the guitar pretty good for being just a kid. Once in a while Granddad would catch me playing his guitar when he came in the room and laugh proudly as I played. He said I was going to be a great musician, and he was going to buy me my own guitar, so when I was home, I could practice and play more often. He said, "You must practice all the time." The way he smiled at me, I knew that he knew, when he left the room, what I was doing — playing his guitar. Maybe that's why he got up and left the room so often; it was his way of sharing it with me.

Granddad's guitar was a real high-quality guitar, and I really shouldn't have been using it. It was so big and heavy; it could easily slip off my knee and fall on the floor and get damaged. On my ninth birthday, after we blew out the candles on the birthday cake Nanny made for me, Granddad surprised me with a guitar of my own. It was a small body electric guitar and it came with a small amplifier, and had its own case. Granddad said I was too young for the kind of guitar he had, so he wanted me to have this one. It wasn't a blonde like his; it was something he called Sunburst. Unlike his guitar, it was shiny and new- looking, like the guitars I saw played by rock and roll groups on the Ed Sullivan show.

My new guitar had what Granddad called "three pickups." Each one, when you pushed the switch in, made the guitar get louder. Another switch made the tone change; it went from a deep bass sound to a high-pitched twangy sound. Granddad said that unlike his guitar, mine was a double cutaway. At the bottom of the neck where it joined the body, it kind of looked like two Mickey Mouse ears — he called the shape a "double cutaway." I took hold of the new guitar, *my* new guitar. On the floor next to the open case was a little brown amplifier; when it was turned on, it had a red glowing light. It had an electric cord that came with the guitar; we plugged one end into the guitar, and the other into the amplifier. I put the guitar on my lap and started to strum the few songs I had memorized as Granddad watched me play. He made me promise to take care of it. He said to wipe it down after I played, with a soft red velvet cloth like he had, to keep away fingerprints and keep the neck of the guitar smooth, just like he did with his guitar. That night when Granddad drove me home, we were both so proud of the new guitar and amplifier. Before he drove away in the old Chevy, he smiled at me and said, "Promise me you're going to practice and take care of it." I didn't have to answer him; my eyes and smile said yes.

As soon as I got the guitar upstairs, I took it out of the case and played until my fingers felt like I got my hand caught in a closing door. Every moment I wasn't in school or out playing in the street with the kids, I was playing my new guitar. My fingers were getting stronger; the more I played, the clearer each note sounded when pressed against the neck. The horrible buzzing sound from a note hit wrong, I heard less now. Even when I watched television while sitting on the floor, my guitar was in my hands, being caressed and strummed. The first thing I did when I came into the apartment, after school, was take my guitar out of the corner, out of the case, and into my hands to practice. I wanted to make Granddad proud of me, and show him that I could keep my promise.

It was now the end of June; my birthday was about a month ago, and I loved that guitar more now then when I first got it. I thought, now that school would be ending soon, I could spend more time practicing. One day after school, I ran up the stairs to get to the apartment, anxious to practice my guitar. I went to the corner where I kept it with the amplifier, and it wasn't there where I left it. I left it in the corner of the living room and boxed it in with the amplifier in front of it, so it couldn't fall and break, even though it was in its case. Nobody was home. I panicked and looked all over the apartment for the guitar. Everywhere I looked — no guitar or amplifier. I ran out of the apartment to look for my mother to see if she knew what happened to my guitar. Where could it be in such a small apartment? How could I not find it? I looked everywhere for it.

I didn't have to go far to find Mom. She was in the bar next to Harry's. I was winded from running, and took deep breaths as I tried to speak to her. I said, "Mom.... Somebody stole my guitar."

She had a drink in one hand, and a cigarette in the other, as she looked down at me. Her eyes were barely open, and in a real calm voice she said,"Your father knows, and he will talk to you about it when he gets home." Even though she didn't say it, I knew something was wrong. She answered me like she knew the answer but didn't want to tell me. I left the bar and went upstairs to the apartment to wait for my father. I looked again all over the apartment, even under the beds this time and behind the couch, as my search got more frantic. My heart was pounding in my chest, and my hands were dripping with sweat. I tried hard not to cry. Every time I swallowed, I could feel a lump in my throat. It seemed like forever waiting there for my father. I couldn't watch television; I paced around the apartment, checking all the places I checked before. I felt like the lions in The Bronx Zoo that went back and forth in their cage. I felt trapped in that apartment.

I heard the door open, and Dad walked in. As I approached him, I couldn't hold back my tears anymore. A flood of tears that I was holding back flowed down my cheeks as I told him my guitar and amplifier were gone. He told me not to cry, and that they were not gone or stolen. He told me that Mom knocked into them while she was vacuuming, and they fell over and broke, and they were being repaired at a music store in Park Chester. Even though we owned a vacuum cleaner, I never saw Mom use it — I never saw her clean the house, so I didn't believe Dad's story. I didn't know what really happened, but I couldn't understand why my father would make up such a story and lie to me. Not only did I love that guitar, but I also made a promise to Granddad to take care of it, and now it was gone. When Granddad asked me if I'm practicing, what would I say? I couldn't lie to him. Even though I hadn't done anything wrong, I felt like I had.

When school finished for the summer, I had promised myself I would practice and practice, and by September, bring in my guitar for show and tell in school. I imagined standing in front of the classroom playing guitar. The boys would look at me with envy, and the girls who didn't find me cute, just might, now that I was a musician. Every day when Dad came home, I asked him about the guitar. When would it be fixed, and when was I going to get it back? I missed playing and practicing music so much. He looked at me, then looked away, as he said, "Soon, real soon." Soon became "We'll see," and that became, "Don't ask me again." He answered me in a way that he became angrier every day as I asked. Two weeks passed, and still no guitar. Now when I asked, he said, "If you ask me again, you're going to get punished." I thought I was already being punished, since I couldn't play guitar anymore.

On weekends, when I was with Granddad, I had to act like I

wasn't interested in playing guitar anymore. I stayed out of his room when he played. I watched cartoons on television, so he wouldn't ask me how I was doing with the guitar. I felt like I disappointed him by not going in his room when he played. I stopped asking my father about the guitar, I didn't want to get punished. For an easy-going man, Dad's voice became threatening if I brought up my guitar. I knew he wasn't telling me the truth by the sound of his voice. Dad usually never talked to me like that.

Weeks passed and I never saw the guitar, so I guess it never got fixed. Without school, and no guitar, the summer days were long. Every day, me and my friends on the block would find things to do — we played stickball, box ball, hide and seek, and rode our bikes. When adventure struck us, we moved to the lots on Lebanon Street, looking for thrown-away treasures. If we were lucky, an abandoned car would show up. Even though the car was old, it would be new to us. We opened the doors and rolled down the windows and sat on the cracked leather bench seats, and for a few days we had a new clubhouse. We weren't the only ones who looked for treasure in the lots. After a few days, our new clubhouse lost its doors, some windows, and all four tires. The hood of the car was usually the first thing that opened, and parts of the motor were taken. By the end of the week, our new clubhouse looked like a Thanksgiving turkey, stripped down and eaten, right down to the bone.

Every day was a new adventure as we shared good times together. When the heat of the midday sun got too unbearable, we took one of the caps off the fire hydrant, and got Harry's big wrench to turn on the water valve on top. Within a few minutes, Lebanon Street was flooded with cool crisp water. We ran through the water with all our clothes on, even our sneakers. We aimed the water flow with a big tin can in front of the hydrant, as we took turns squirting each other with this powerful cannon of water. We stuffed up the sewers, so the water couldn't drain, and made a pond that rose from the street to the top of the concrete sidewalk. The old ladies that sat on beach chairs outside the buildings laughed at us as we ran through the water, cooling off.

I'm sure years ago, when they were our age, they did the same thing. Not much changes in The Bronx. My friend Kevin, who lived in my building, didn't join in when we got wild like this. He watched us from his apartment window. The way he waved and smiled at us, you could see he wanted to.

Kevin and his brother Matt had strict parents who took them to church a lot. They were always better-dressed than we were, too. The boys never cursed, and wore shoes instead of sneakers. They went to Catholic school and wore suits and carried briefcases like little businessmen. Whenever I saw Kevin and his brother Matt outside playing in front of the building, I joined them in whatever they wanted to do, since they were also my friends. Kevin was my age, but taller. Matt was a big chubby kid. He was thirteen, but looked much older. He looked old enough to drive, but he walked everywhere. He never played sports with us, and just by the way he walked, you knew he couldn't run, and had never swung a baseball bat. Even though he had a lisp when he spoke, he loved to talk. Some words came out wrong when he got excited as he told stories about anything military. For some reason he loved talking about soldiers and armies and war. With his allowance, instead of spending it in Harry's candy store on toys, once a week he walked down Tremont Avenue toward Fordham Road to the old Army and Navy store. Each week he came home with something from that store. He loved to collect Army medals and canteens. He had bullets and Army knives and helmets that the soldiers wore in combat. He even wore a soldier's belt around his waist that had survival tools clipped to it. I didn't know anything about the Army or wars, but when Matt told you stories, his big blue eyes lit up like a rocket in the night sky. If you stood close to him when he told his stories, his lisp speckled your face with a few drops of spit.

One day, he told me that tomorrow he and Kevin were walking down to Fordham Road to the Army and Navy store to look at some old guns and bayonets and Army gear. I was never in that store, but I liked spending time with the brothers, so I told him to call for me before they went, and I would go with them. The next day came, and

Kevin and Matt knocked on my door. We left the building and walked down Tremont Avenue toward Fordham Road. I was never up this far off the block before, but Kevin and Matt knew the way. They were my guides through a jungle of new stores. As we walked together, we looked at all the windows that had toys and bikes and sports stuff. After a few blocks we found an Italian ice place, and for fifty cents, all three of us walked out with a lemon ice.

As we walked and talked and licked our ices, Matt said, "There's a cool pawn shop on the corner with all kinds of cool stuff to look at." The sign was big enough to see from down the block, it had three balls around the word "PAWN." We stopped to look in the windows that took up the whole corner. In the windows you could see all the items they were selling. There were watches, rings, and jewelry. There were television sets and stereos, bikes and trumpets and saxophones. There were drums and a piano in the window. Up high in the window on a rack, hanging off a hook, was something I never thought I would see again.... My guitar. I KNOW IT'S MINE, even though there were a lot of guitars hanging next to it on both sides, I KNOW IT'S MINE. I played it for hours day after day and cleaned every inch of it with the red velvet cloth Granddad gave me. I know the shiny Sunburst color, that started out black, and then faded to brown until the brown became yellow like the sun. It was the only guitar hanging there with the three pickups, and the double cutaway that looked like Mickey Mouse ears where the neck joined the body. Hanging off the neck at the top near the strings was a white tag with a dollar sign, and one hundred written in numbers. I know it's mine, but there's nothing I could do about it. It just hung there, next to the other guitars, not special anymore. I wondered how they all got there. What stories did the parents tell those kids who were missing their guitars like I was?

As I looked up at the guitar, I got that same lump in my throat like I was about to cry, but I couldn't. I never told the brothers that the guitar in the window was mine. I was afraid they would think that I was making it up. Matt liked to tell stories, but this was one story I didn't want to tell anybody. I didn't want to ever leave that window. I kept looking at my guitar just hanging there. I remembered the story about the genie in the lamp, and how the genie gave you three wishes. I wanted only one wish. I would've given the other two wishes to Kevin and Matt. My only wish would have been to find one hundred dollars, and walk out of that store with my guitar. As I stood in front of the window, a push from Kevin and "Let's go" from Matt signaled the last time I would ever see my guitar. We continued to walk to the old Army and Navy store for Matt, so he could get some new cool Army stuff. I didn't mean to stop talking to Matt and Kevin. I just felt different than I had before I saw the guitar.

After going through all the boxes in the Army and Navy store, Matt spent his two dollars on an Army knife that had a spoon and a can opener in it, and clipped it on his belt. We walked back down Tremont Avenue to go home. As we walked, Matt made up new stories about the soldier who used his knife. When I got to the apartment, I turned on the television and watched cartoons. I glanced over to the corner where my guitar used to be. It looked much better there than in the window of the pawn shop. I never told my parents where I'd been, and what I saw, or what I knew. All I knew was ... I didn't want them to lie to me again. Even though I'm just a kid, they should know better!

You Gotta Believe

EVEN THOUGH NANNY didn't go to church, she was very spiritual and believed in God. After she said most things, she would end the sentence by saying, "God be willing." Most things she would ask for were not for herself; she always wanted good things to be the outcome, and always asked for God's approval. She had a St. Christopher medal that she kept in her drawer. It was blessed by a priest at Saint Theresa's church, up on the Avenue. She told me I was old enough, so she gave it to me, and told me to wear it on the thin silver chain that was already on it. She told me, "You gotta believe," and that if I prayed to God and held the medal in my hand, my prayers would be answered, but only if I believed in God, and in what I was praying for. She said if I wanted something to happen, I should pray for it to happen and believe that it would, and with enough prayer and belief, it would come true.

At seven years old, I didn't understand how holding a medal of the saint, and thinking about what I wanted, and deeply believing it, would make it come true. To me, this sounded like magic – to "believe," and it would come true. That was magic. At seven, I believed in magic. On TV, there were magicians who made the impossible come true. After all, a rabbit came out of a hat — the same hat that, a few minutes ago, water came out of, and birds flew out of. All it took was a magician to wave a magic wand above the hat, and the rabbit even disappeared. It happened that way because the magician thought really hard and believed it would happen, and he prayed to Abra Cadabra.

On July fourth, The Bronx Street where I lived sounded like a war zone. The older kids, the teenagers, shot off fireworks to celebrate the day. It was loud and festive, with a flash of light followed by the thunderous Kaboom! of the fireworks, which shook the ground as they went off. As the fireworks were being thrown on the ground, they went off with a bang, but once in a while, after they were lit and thrown, nothing would happen. The kids called this a "dud." Me and the other kids my age that didn't have fireworks would run over to the fireworks that didn't go off, and collect the duds. We would collect handfuls of duds, and throw them into a small fire that was in the middle of the street. Once in the fire, the gunpowder ignited with a flash of light that amused all of us little kids who didn't have fireworks.

Big Carlo was lighting off and throwing firecrackers by the pack, like all the teenagers that night. After the firecrackers went off, I ran over to pick through the ones that didn't go off, so I could collect them, and throw them into the fire. I ran to pick through and collect the duds. I got on my knees to inspect the firecrackers. I picked up a whole bunch of duds that didn't go off. As I reached down, I found another firecracker dud for my collection. I didn't notice that the fuse was still lit, and with a bang, and a flash of fire, it went off, and exploded while it was in my hand near my chest as I held it. The flash of fire from the explosion bloodied my fingers and tore through my shirt and burned my chest. Scared and hurt, I ran crying upstairs to my apartment to get my parents' help and consolation. When I got upstairs, no one was home.

As I cried and felt the skin on my chest burning and bleeding, I saw that the St. Christopher's medal Nanny gave me was pressed against the charred skin on my chest. As I cried in the dark apartment, all alone, I heard Nanny's voice in my head telling me to hold the medal and pray, and I did. I held the medal and prayed that Nanny was here to help me. I close my eyes and held the medal and prayed, and I believed my prayers would be answered, and Nanny would come to help me. At seven years old, it was a simple prayer: "Nanny,

I'm hurt, come help me, I need you," over and over, as I rocked back and forth and held the St. Christopher medal in my hand. I noticed it was the same hand that was bleeding at my fingertips that had held the firecracker. Over and over for what seemed like forever, I repeated my simple prayer. I was so sure that Nanny believed in God and prayer, so I did, too — I had to believe this, because Nanny told me so. I knew she would come for me, and help me. I sat in the dark holding my bloody chest and the St. Christopher medal tightly in my bleeding hand. I sat on the windowsill in the living room and looked out the window so I could see Nanny when she pulled up in Granddad's black-and-white Chevy Biscayne.

Like a small miracle, the car did come soon; the car horn was beeping and before it came to a stop, I was on my feet and running out the door, down the stairs to the car to show Nanny what had happened. We both held each other and cried. I asked her how she knew what had happened and that I needed her. She said she felt something was wrong, and she knew I was in trouble, and God asked her to come here and help me. She told me, "You prayed for me to come and God granted your prayer because you believed it with all your heart. You have to believe in your prayers, and they will come true."

I knew this "believe" thing was magical, and somehow, that day, it worked, and I too became a magician. I understood now that when Nanny said "You gotta believe," you just gotta believe.

Edgar Flies

THE PEOPLE WHO lived on Morris Park and Tremont Avenue in The Bronx where I lived were mostly blue-collar white people. In the surrounding areas just a few blocks from here, near West Farms and down Tremont Avenue, the neighborhood changed. It was a mixture of white, black, and Hispanic people. The first Hispanic family to join our neighborhood was Edgar's. Edgar was a dark handsome boy with ebony-black hair and a perfect smile. He had ivory-white teeth that looked even whiter against his dark skin. Edgar was a few years older than me, but he was younger than the bigger kids, who were teenagers.

Even though there were clearly two age groups on the block, we all played together on Lebanon Street. When we picked teams for stickball, football, or hide and seek, we mixed it up equally between both age groups. When we chose sides for teams, street etiquette was that captains picked one big guy and one little guy, to make it fair. You couldn't have the teenagers against the kids my age. What would be the fun or challenge of that? Any game would be over in just a few minutes, with a whopping uneven scoreboard. Skill level and age work hand-in-hand in sports and street games.

Edgar, being bigger than my size, got thrown in as a big kid, even though he wasn't one. That set Edgar's ranking in the kids' community. He was a big kid now. Edgar had to try harder all the time to keep his "big kid" status. He ran faster, and swung the bat harder at every ball. He slid into all bases in stickball, so he wouldn't be called out.

He had a tough time filling big sneakers with a little foot. After everything he did, Edgar always flashed his movie star smile and said, "No big thing," confidently, even though it probably was. The pressure of being one of the big kids never seemed to bother him. He had the swagger of a sixteen-year-old at twelve.

On weekends, the kids in the neighborhood stayed out all day and into the night. Edgar was no exception. He fit in from the first day he arrived on the block. I was one of the younger kids, and I usually went upstairs to the apartment when it got dark. The next day on the street, the younger kids like me would find out what had gone on with the older kids last night. We listened with our ears perked up, like the dog sitting in front of the old record player, being schooled with every word. After all, soon it would be our turn to be the teenagers on the block. They talked about hanging out at Harry's candy store until it closed. They told us how they would go with the girls into the lots on Lebanon Street and make out. Edgar was part of that group. He didn't have a father to tell him when he was to go upstairs for the night. He had no rules; his mother couldn't control him.

Sometimes during the day, we saw Edgar's mother and little sister leaving Bernie's grocery store. She walked with a grocery bag in one hand, and Edgar's sister held the other. His mother and sister always wore colorful dresses and looked dressed-up. They had beautiful dark hair like Edgar, and shy smiles, unlike Edgar's confident grin. His sister was very young, maybe four or five years old. I never saw her in the street playing, like other girls her age. When we saw Edgar's mother and sister, they walked to him and they spoke to him in Spanish, so we had no idea what they spoke about. Edgar just smiled and answered his mother tenderly in a soft voice and stroked his sister's hair, and then he kissed his mother goodbye at the end of their talk. He was the only kid on the block who kissed his mother in front of everybody. It was nice to see that!

The big kids on the block talked about how they were getting high at night. They said they bought tubes of glue from Harry's candy store — the glue we used to put together our models. They squeezed the glue into a bag, and put the bag to their mouths and noses and breathed it in. They called it "huffing." They said at night they "huffed" in the lots, or up on the roof, where they couldn't be seen by adults. They all said "it was cool and it felt good getting high."

Edgar was one of the big kids, so he hung out with the big kids that got high by "huffing" glue. Edgar stopped playing stickball during the day with us. Instead, during the day he "huffed" glue and walked around high most of the time. After a while, I didn't see his confident smile anymore. He stumbled around the neighborhood, high all the time. His eyes were bloodshot and he giggled to himself like he was in another world, and he found everything funny. He was high so often that the kids stayed away from him, since his behavior was getting strange and he didn't welcome our friendship anymore. He wasn't the Edgar we knew as our friend. We all felt uneasy around him.

Now, if you saw him in the street and went over to him, instead of a smile and an arm around your shoulder, he said, "Give me some money, empty your pockets, let me see what you got." Kids my age didn't feel the same around him anymore, and the big kids took advantage of him when he was high. They pushed him around and punched him in the arms and chest with "get away from us" punches. All bullies like a kid like Edgar, who didn't punch back. He couldn't fight back; he was too high to defend himself. Whenever Edgar came around, the punches got thrown more easily. Sometimes he was pushed to the ground, and he rolled around laughing while he was on his back trying to get up. In my neighborhood, his weakness allowed the big kids to treat him like a human punching bag. It was sad to see Edgar like this. He didn't join in our games anymore, and he stopped fitting in.

One weekend, while I was at Nanny's house, the big kids, the teenagers, beat Edgar up pretty bad. When I saw him on Monday after school, he had a black eye and a bruise above his lip. I asked him, "What happened to you? Were you in a fight?"

He put his head down and said, "They beat me up — it was no fight. I was high, and you can't fight high."

I got closer to him. I wanted to put my hand on him, to let him know I was sorry for him, and still his friend. He pushed me away and told me to mind my own business. He said, "You're just a kid." So was he — or did he forget? I always liked Edgar, so whenever I saw him on the block, I went over to him. Before I could sit down next to him as he sat on the sidewalk, he told me, "Go away, leave me alone." After a while, I did. I just waved to him, even though he never waved back. What I missed most about Edgar was his confident smile. He didn't smile much anymore; all he wanted to do was get high. All the kids on the block picked on him, and made fun of him as he stumbled around when he was high.

Most weekends, I went to Nanny's house. My dad drove me over when he had a car. If he didn't, on Friday after school, I used my bus pass and got to Nanny's house with two bus rides. I stayed over until Sunday night, when Granddad drove me home. Some nights I had to wait until *The Lawrence Welk Show* was over. Granddad was a musician, and liked to listen to the big band sound of Lawrence Welk, and he hated to miss that show. Some nights I waited until *The Ed Sullivan Show* was over. It depended on what Granddad wanted to watch while I sat beside him.

Granddad pulled up in front of the building; I ran up the stairs and waved to him when I got in the apartment. When he saw me at the window, he beeped goodbye and drove away. Once I was upstairs in the apartment, I fell asleep on the couch with the television on. I slept on the couch through the night. My dad woke me in the morning and said he was going to work. He gave me two dollars and told me not to fall back asleep. He said, "Get to Harry's and go to school; I'll see you later."

In the same clothes I slept in, I walked downstairs to Harry's candy store to get a chocolate doughnut and milk; and for Mom, coffee, French cruller, and cigarettes. If she woke up during the day, she would look for them. That was my job before I went to school. As soon as I walked into Harry's, I saw my friends Paulie and Skinny Mary. They ran to me. "Did you hear what happened to Edgar?"

"No, what?" I said.

Mary's chin and lower lip came forward and shook as she spoke. She was trying not to cry. She said, "He was huffing glue on the roof — he got so high he fell off."

I looked at her. I couldn't say anything. After a moment, without thinking, I asked, "Is he okay?" How could anyone fall off a six-story roof and be okay? They said he was dead. They told me he was on the roof getting high, and he stuck his head over the side and started to yell down to the teenagers. Then he got on the roof ledge and started to walk along the roof, like a guy in the circus on a tight rope. They said he walked and shouted down, "I'm flying...I'm flying," while he laughed. The kids on the street yelled back, "Get off the roof, you'll fall!" A moment later he stumbled and his arms were waving like he was trying to catch his balance. He fell off the roof, onto the street, to his death.

I couldn't believe what I heard. I couldn't speak to them. I wanted to cry, but held back. I knew if I did cry they'd call me a baby. That's what we all did to each other on the block. It was so cruel that we couldn't show emotion at a moment like this, without being called names. So I just stood there, in silence. I walked over to the counter as Harry stood behind it. He acted like nothing was wrong. He said, "What you want, kid?"

I said, "Harry, I take the same thing every day; you know what I want." He looked at me like I was being fresh with him. I could tell by the way he squinted his eyes at me. I wasn't being fresh; I just wasn't myself after hearing about Edgar. I took the paper bag Harry handed me upstairs to the apartment. I left the bag on the right side table near Mom as she snored and slept with her eyes half- open. I didn't take out my doughnut or chocolate milk. I couldn't eat; I couldn't think about anything but Edgar. I really liked Edgar; he was part of our neighborhood. He was one of my friends, and now he was dead. How could he do such a thing? I couldn't believe he was dead, and I'd never see him again. When you're a kid, you always think you'll see each other forever. That's why we never said "goodbye," we always said, "see you later."

I knew I wouldn't see Edgar later. I knew I'd miss his confident smile — the one he had before he started getting high. His mother and sister moved away a week after he died. No one on the block ever talked about Edgar again. We never spoke about what he did, or how he died. It was like he was never there, like he was never one of us. Most of the kids on the block that did get high stopped. All the little kids my age never started. We didn't want to wind up like Edgar. It was selfish to think like that, but his death taught us how to live. Harry never sold glue at his candy store anymore. He sold only cars and airplane models that snapped together. Edgar's death changed all of us, even Harry.

Two Sewer Homeruns

STICKBALL WAS A great event in The Bronx, and we could all play, even though we were all not the same age. There were two teams, just like baseball. The players of the teams changed every day. Two of the older boys, usually somebody's brothers, would call "captain." Then, one by one, the captains would choose who was on their team, as they alternately picked from the kids who were standing there and waiting to play. Since we all played together daily, we knew who the best and who the worst players were.

There were usually five people on each team, and the game was played on Lebanon Street. The street was very long, but very narrow. It was about two car lengths wide, and on each side of the street there were parked cars. The parked cars served as first base and third base. Home plate was the round sewer cover in the street. Second base was the next sewer cover, about fifty feet on a straight line from home plate. Beyond that sewer cover, about 100 feet farther out, was another sewer cover. Any ball that hit two sewers was a home run. If the ball was hit that far, you didn't have to run the bases — it was an automatic home run — unless you wanted to. The rooftops on either side of the street were an out, and if you hit it up there, you had to go on the roof to get the ball. If the ball hit a building and you caught it off the building, it was out. When the ball was hit to the side of a parked car, you had to use your judgment to play it off the angles.

The game of stickball was loosely fashioned around real baseball. This was The Bronx version of baseball. There were no gloves, no uniforms — just a ball, and a broomstick for a bat. This was stickball. To get our equipment we would go down to one of the basements of the apartment buildings and find an old broom or mop. Then we would bring the broom back to the street. To make the broom a bat for the stickball game, we had to cut off the top. Since we had no tools to do so, we would lift up the sewer top and put the broom under the sewer top and drop the heavy iron top of the sewer to cut off the broom head. The sewer top was so heavy that we all had to work together to lift it up without dropping it on our feet to get a clean cut and separate the broom from the stick as we dropped the sewer top on it. Now we had a stickball bat. If the stick came out splintered or rough around the edges, we would scratch it smooth on the concrete sidewalk like it was sandpaper.

Now the ball. To kids in The Bronx, the Spaldeen (Spalding) pink balls were like currency; your wealth was measured on how many balls you carried. All of us had at least a few balls that we carried in our jeans pockets. Now we had to select the best ball. The one that bounced the highest was chosen. The owner of the ball would always call "chips." Chips meant that if the ball was lost during the game, the kids playing the game had to chip in to buy a new ball to replace it. That meant the ball WAS as valuable as money.

With bat and ball in place, now we picked the team players. We were all picked by size, age, and ranking in the stickball community. The good players were always picked first. Since I was a good player, I was never picked last, and that made me feel good. If you couldn't catch or hit, you ranked low, and were the last man picked on the team. Even at such an early age, we had the science of hitting the ball perfected. I was a two-bounce and swing kid. Some kids just threw it up and hit it on the fly. I always hit past the second base sewer, and sometimes even a two-sewer home run. When fielding, I wasn't afraid of the ball, and caught everything.

We played stickball for hours; usually the same team would stick together for the whole day even after we took short breaks at Harry's candy store. Whoever had the most wins out of three games was the champion team of the day. We never had a rivalry or badmouthed each other, because we knew tomorrow we could be teammates. When the game was over, we all went to Harry's candy store for lime rickey (seltzer, lime syrup, and cherry syrup). We put on our tough-kid faces as we entered Harry's because we knew we would have to walk past Johnny Moon, and he would stare at you until you said his name out of respect, which got you his nod of approval to enter to Harry's without a problem. The lime rickeys went down better with Devil Dogs, and "Sugar Shack" was on the jukebox. Big Alice (Harry's daughter) smiled and flirted with the older boys from the block while standing behind the counter. Even though I'm just a kid, it felt good being part of a team, and living on such a great block, in such a great neighborhood.

Christmas Shopping at Robert Hall's

IT'S A FEW weeks before Christmas and I'm watching Channel 11 with Officer Joe Bolton and The Three Stooges. Moe just finished poking Curly in the eye, and ripped out a handful of Larry's hair. Officer Joe breaks for a commercial. A commercial with a catchy jingle comes on; it's a woman and her family walking into a clothing store. She starts to sing, "We're doing our Christmas shopping at Robert Hall's today." Over the last few days, I heard my mother and father say they were going to do their Christmas shopping at Robert Hall's in Park Chester. On every commercial break, that catchy jingle for Robert Hall's clothing store was played. Being overwhelmed with the Christmas spirit and that catchy jingle, my mother and father looked at each other and started to sing the jingle. They sang it differently, though. They sang, "We're doing our Christmas copping at Robert Halls today." They changed shopping to copping — it rhymed well enough, but I couldn't figure out why they changed the words in the commercial. As long as Mom and Dad got the Christmas spirit and went shopping, who cared if they sang it with a few words wrong?

As Christmas got closer, the days passed by quickly. Today was Thursday, and as the commercial sang to us all week long, a voice came at the end and said, "Don't miss the Big Sale this Thursday at Robert Hall's — and remember, we're open till midnight on Thursday." As I ate Campbell's chicken and rice soup for dinner, my mother told me that tonight they were going out shopping. She said they would lock me in, and I should watch TV on the couch until I fell asleep, and when they came home Dad would carry me into bed. They sang the Robert Hall's jingle as they put their coats on. They sang their version of the Robert Hall's jingle,"We're doing our Christmas copping at Robert Hall's tonight," as they laughed and amused each other.

Dad put on his old black leather jacket and Mom wore her long cloth coat with her special shopping bag hung over her arm. This was the same bag she always shopped with. This bag looked like a small rug folded in half with leather straps. As they left the apartment, Dad said, "Be a good boy and don't unlock the door; we'll see you later after we go shopping." They left the apartment, and I could hear the lock on the door turn from the outside with a key as they locked me in. I watched a lot of TV, and lay across the couch with a pillow and blanket. By about nine o'clock, I couldn't keep my eyes open any longer, and I fell asleep. It didn't feel like I had been sleeping very long when I heard the door open and my parents come into the apartment. As they came down the hall and into the living room, they were laughing and singing their version of the Robert Hall's song. Again they changed the words. They sang, "We did our Christmas copping at Robert Hall's this year."

Their laughing and singing woke me, as they stumbled into the dark living room. They turned on the two big lamps to view all the clothes they got tonight at Robert Hall's on their shopping spree. As my eyes focused, I could see that Dad had on a new black leather jacket, and Mom had a new coat also. Instead of the long cloth coat she left with, she too had a black leather coat, a long one, almost down to her ankles. The both of them looked so good in their new leather coats. They looked almost like the people in the commercial. Then Mom turned her big bag upside down on the couch next to me. Out came shirts, socks, gloves, sweaters, pants, slippers, and even three watches. As she shook it all out, it piled high on the couch. It was unbelievable how much stuff came out of her bag. Mom's bag was like Felix the Cat's magic bag. Anything and everything fell out of Felix's bag when he opened it up, just like Mom's. Before tonight, I never saw the resemblance between Mom and Felix the Cat, but now I did.

In this pile there looked like there was something for everyone in my family. This was truly going to be a merry Christmas. Nothing came in shopping bags, and all the sweaters and shirts still had tags on them. Even the coat that my dad wore out of the store had a tag tucked inside the sleeve, just like Mom's. I saw cowboy pajamas for me, even though I didn't ask for them. They looked warm and comfortable, so I was happy to see them. Both Mom and Dad looked over all they brought back from Robert Hall's, and talked to each other in whispered voices.

I overheard Dad say to Mom, "You got that in the wrong size; weren't you watching what you were doing?"

She answered back, "It's not easy getting all this with one eye getting, and one eye watching out, and I had to get for everybody, while you just got yourself that leather jacket."

She told Dad whatever was wrong, she'd take it back tomorrow and tell the cashier she got the wrong size and exchange it, and tell her she forgot the receipt. She said, "It'll work; it always does."

Now that I was awake, I didn't have to be carried into the bedroom that we shared. I put the blanket over my shoulder and carried my pillow into the bedroom to sleep for the night. In the morning before school, I walked back into the living room to look at all the clothes they got for Christmas one more time. Before I went to school I went to Harry's candy store to get breakfast for myself, and cigarettes, coffee, and a French cruller for Mom while she slept.

Today was Friday, and after school on most Fridays I went to Nanny's house for the weekend. I had to take two buses just to get there. I took one bus that was across the street from my building on Tremont Avenue, and the other bus on Westchester Square to get to Nanny's. I had my school bus pass, so I showed it to the bus drivers while getting on the buses. I had to carry my books with me, so they thought I was coming home from school and I lived there. I'm only eight years old, but I'm big for my age, so I always hoped the bus drivers wouldn't ask me where I was going. All through dinner at Nanny's house, I was excited over the Christmas shopping Mom and Dad did.

I overheard them say they had a sweater and gloves for Granddad and a sweater and slippers for Nanny. I told Nanny how they locked me in and sang the Robert Hall song before and after they went shopping. As I sang the song the way they did — "We're doing our Christmas copping at Robert Hall's this year" — she rolled her eyes and opened her mouth before I could finish the song.

She said, "It's shopping, not copping. Copping is a bad word. It means to steal — it means you take things and don't pay for them. Is that the way they sang it?" she asked.

I didn't answer her. Now, it all made sense to me why Mom and Dad changed the words to the song ... all the tags still on everything, no shopping bags, the labels and price tags still on the coats as they wore them into the apartment. Also, the Felix the Cat magic bag Mom emptied out on the couch. Unlike the song, they didn't "shop"; they "copped." They stole all those clothes and watches from the Robert Hall store. That's why they waited for Thursday — it was sale night, late night, when lots of people were in the store and nobody could watch what they did. That's what Mom meant when she said, "It's not easy getting all this with one eye." She was looking around to make sure no one saw her stealing as she put things in her bag.

Even though I loved Nanny, I couldn't tell her what I had just figured out, and I didn't want to get Mom and Dad in trouble. Even though I'm just a kid, I know being a tattletale isn't good either. I also figured out that the only time they got along with each other, laughing and singing like they did, was when they did bad things together. Just like that time at the Chinese restaurant. Even though Christmas was coming, I didn't want the cowboy pajamas anymore.

Not One Bus, but Two

WHILE DAD WORKED, and I was in school, Mom was sleeping, or at the bar. Her next favorite thing to do was shoplift. Since Mom couldn't drive and the Rambler was gone, she would take the bus to Fordham Road in The Bronx to shoplift. Her favorite store to plunder was Alexander's. Alexander's was a huge department store. There were no anti-theft measures in place. There were no guards at the front doors. There were no plastic security tags that had to be removed. Shoppers were on the honor system. If you saw something that you liked, you brought it to the cash register to pay for it.

Mom had a world-class shoplifting bag that she wore over her left arm. The bag looked like an oriental rug folded in half, with big leather straps for handles. When she opened the bag, her right hand would fill it with anything from clothes to jewelry or perfumes. She stole anything she wanted, anything that the store employees took their eyes off of for a moment. She did this usually twice a week. Dad never seemed to mind, because she never spent money on clothes and accessories, and she usually came home with something for me and Dad too. The black leather jacket Dad wore every day was Mom's Alexander's parting gift. I had cowboy pajamas that Alexander gave me, but mostly she stole for herself. In her closet and dresser drawers, there were still labels on all of her clothes.

One day after school, after Harry's, after box ball, I went upstairs and Mom wasn't there. I thought she was at the bar or somewhere she didn't want to be found. This happened so often that didn't pay any mind to it. I just watched cartoons, and soon Dad would be home from work. When Dad did come home and Mom wasn't around, he went to look for her. He looked in the bar and she wasn't there. He went to Eleanor's apartment — she was Mom's drinking buddy — but she wasn't there. He came home without her, and she never came home that night. Dad worried a little, but it wasn't the first time she didn't come home.

We both went to bed. When I woke up, Dad was already gone; he went to work. Mom was still missing. I went to Harry's and charged my doughnut and chocolate milk for breakfast, and went to school. After school, still no Mom. I checked the bar when I got off the school bus, and walked down Morris Park Avenue. I checked the storefronts in front of the building before I went upstairs. She wasn't at Frank the fruit man's, she wasn't at Bernie's, she wasn't at Aldo's dry cleaners, and she wasn't at Jimmy Moy's. No sign of her anywhere, no Mom.

That night as Dad and I were on the couch watching TV, the phone rang, and it was Mom. She said she was in the hospital on Fordham Road. Since we had no car, Dad and I took a taxi to see her in the hospital. When we came into the room, she was sitting up in bed. We were both shocked by her appearance and her attitude. She didn't seem like someone who was happy to be alive after what just happened. Even though she was bruised, she was angry, and cursed when she spoke. She said, "That stupid bus driver hit me; when I get out of here; I'm going to find out who he is and kill him."

I'd seen Mom walk out of our neighborhood bar many times; her steps and direction couldn't be calculated by anyone, especially not a bus driver, on a busy street with a busload of passengers, making change and taking fares. How was he to know this crazy, stumbling lady was going to walk across the street as he drove by? As with everything she did, it wasn't her fault – at least, not according to her. She was so black and blue that she looked purple all over her body — her arms, her legs, even her face. Her body was a rainbow of colored bruises. She was blue and yellow and purple, like the right side of a box of crayons.

She told us that after she spent the afternoon shopping at Alexander's; after she filled her bag, it was too early to go home, so she had a few drinks at a nearby bar so she wouldn't be thirsty on the bus ride home. After a few drinks, she left the bar and she was crossing the street to catch the bus to get home. She said she stepped off the curb and a bus hit her, throwing her up in the air, and while she was in the air, another bus, going in the opposite direction, hit her after she bounced off the windshield of the first bus. She went flying in the air and landed on the sidewalk across the street, on the opposite sidewalk from where she stepped off. The way she described it, it sounded like the buses were playing Ping-Pong with her, and she was the ball. Being hit by the second bus probably saved her life. Had she been hit only by the first bus, the oncoming cars would have run her over. So her being lifted off the ground and landing on the opposite sidewalk was what probably saved her.

As I looked at her all purple in the bed, for some reason I couldn't go near her. She scared me. Maybe it was because I wasn't used to seeing her that color, or she didn't act like she wanted any sympathy. She was loud and cursed a lot. My father didn't have much to say to her either. As we left her room and walked down the hospital stairs, my father said, "God watches over bums and drunks." That day, God added " thieves" to his list. That's how Mom's life was spared from being killed that day. Not many people survive being hit by a bus. Even fewer people are still alive after being hit by two buses.

After a week in the hospital, Mom wasn't so purple anymore; she was different shades of yellow, like the left side of a crayon box. She was released from the hospital, and took a taxi back to the apartment while Dad worked, and I was in school. As soon as she was able to walk to the bus stop on Tremont Avenue, she returned to Alexander's on Fordham Road, and took advantage of her no-cash purchases and five-finger discounts. You would think that after what she went through, a lesson would be learned by this miracle, her still being alive, but it wasn't. Even I got the message, and I'm not a grown-up like Mom...I'm just a kid.

The Elevator

MY BUILDING AT 437 Morris Park Avenue had an elevator. We were the only building in the neighborhood that did. All the other buildings on Lebanon Street were what we called walkups. I lived on the fourth floor. Since I had an elevator, I had three choices: wait, ride, or run. If I was in the lobby and pushed the button for the elevator, why wait to get upstairs to the apartment? I knew by the time the elevator came down to the lobby, I could "beat it" upstairs to the fourth floor. Sometimes, it didn't make any sense to stand in the lobby and wait for the slow elevator, especially since I could run up the steps two at a time, leaping left foot to right, holding the banister for speed, as I mastered the steps like rocks in a riverbed. The elevator was like the building — old, and broken a lot.

There were plenty of kids in the building, and all the kids, including me, learned how to make the old broken elevator even more broken. We called it "stickin' the elevator." The way it works was, once you were inside the elevator and the elevator door closed, you pressed down all the buttons on the panel at the exact same time. The old elevator didn't know what floor you wanted, so it just stayed there, stuck. The other way to stick the elevator was, once it was moving, going up to a floor, and wedging your fingers between the door after it closed. Then you would push back on the door in the direction it opened, and the elevator stopped, thinking it was at a floor. Once the elevator was stuck in that position between floors, you opened the door back all the way, and pushed open the door for the floor below, then bellied down and wiggled out. You could also open the door above to the next floor, and climb up, out of the elevator. Both options could be very dangerous. Sometimes the elevator wasn't high enough or low enough to allow the door above or below to open. Once the elevator recognized the problem, the door closed automatically and squeezed you like a vise, between the closing door and the side of the elevator. Oh, what fun!!!

Once the elevator was stuck like this, after you climbed out, it didn't work again until the super (Bronx for superintendent) came to fix it. In my neighborhood, our super was an older man — a short, round, gray-haired man named Bruno. Bruno was not only the "super," he was a friend of my mom's. Often during the day, he came up to our apartment to fix things, and drink with my mother, before she got dressed to go out to the bar. I think Bruno drank more than he fixed. He was also attracted to my mom; I could tell by the way he looked at her. She was much younger than him, and clearly more attractive than his own wife. His wife lived in a house dress and had a broom stuck in her hands. I never saw her without her broom. Maybe she was a witch.

Mom could get Bruno to do anything. He was a willing victim for any of her half-baked plans. Like the time Bruno put shelves over the dumbwaiter, and the time he cut a hole through the kitchen wall, so Mom could pass the food she never cooked through it to the living room while I watched television.

Bruno and his family lived in the basement of the building. All day long he managed to find something to do, something to fix, or someone to share a glass of wine with. He was a cheerful man and smiled a lot, even though he had no teeth. His round face and toothless smile made him look innocent, like a chubby baby. During the downtime when the elevator was broken, everybody had to take the stairs and walk upstairs to get to their apartment. It was a stupid and thoughtless thing for us to do, but we all "stuck" the elevator, and we all bragged about it. We never considered the people that had groceries and had to climb the steps up to the fifth or sixth floor. There were old people in my building too, and with the elevator broken, they remained "stuck" in their apartments, just like the elevator. When you have young legs, you don't know how old legs feel climbing up and down those steps. It wasn't nice that the older people were stuck in their apartment, but we did it anyway.

The elevator always eventually got fixed by Bruno. It wasn't long before me or one of us kids who lived in the building "stuck" it again. Being able to stick an elevator and climb out was another Bronx rite of passage. When you were old enough to stick an elevator, somehow on the streets, now you were old enough for lots of things. It was a secret that was passed down from the older kids to the younger kids in the building, like me. I knew when I got older, I had to pass down "stickin' the elevator," to the next generation of kids coming up. It was one of the secrets that we shared in the bad kid world.

Our parents never knew it was the kids who stuck the elevator. They all cursed the old building, and the old elevator. If only they really knew.... Elevator antics didn't stop here. When there were two of us in the elevator, after we stuck the elevator between floors, we climbed on each other's shoulders and out the escape hatch on the ceiling of the elevator. Now we were riding on top of the elevator in-side the elevator shaft as it went up and down. When I did it, I saw the cables and big metal weights that moved the elevator from one floor to the next. It was almost like a science project. I learned about cables and pulleys and saw the hydraulic motor that moved the elevator up and down. Hey, education is education, however you get it. This was very dangerous, but also thrilling at the same time, riding on top of the elevator. It was dirty and slippery under our feet. At any time, one of us could have slipped and fallen to the bottom of the elevator shaft. Since the building was six stories high, falling off from riding on top of the elevator would have been a long and deadly fall before we splat-tered to the bottom. I'm sure no one could survive such a fall, but we took the risk anyway, without thinking … just like the kids before us. We weren't the pioneers of cable riding. Danger and excitement went hand-in-hand once the challenge of sticking the elevator was over, so riding the cables was only natural.

Whenever Mom or Dad came home and they told me they had to take the stairs because the old elevator was broken, I laughed to myself because I knew the truth. I knew what had happened. That poor elevator got a bad reputation for being unreliable, and Bruno the super got a bad reputation for not knowing how to fix it.

Hey, I'm just a kid — even though what I did in the elevator wasn't smart, sometimes your brain gets "STUCK" between floors on the way up to being a big kid!

Everybody Loves You
When You're Down and Out

IT WAS A hot July afternoon. It must have been about four o'clock, because Mom was still in the bar. She had to get out of the bar before five o'clock, so my father wouldn't get off the train and catch her in the bar, drinking, and flirting with the men who didn't seem to work. When he got off the train after work, he had to pass the bar on Morris Park Avenue to get to the apartment. He always checked the bar for Mom. A few times I saw him drag her out by her arm, lifting her off the ground with each step she took. Another time, he dragged her out by the back of her hair as she cursed him, and fought to get away, while everybody in the bar looked on.

On the days she wasn't sleeping, she would go to the bar in the afternoon. The bar was next to Harry's candy store, and since I was always at Harry's or playing in front of Harry's, I would look in on her from time to time. I knew she'd had too much to drink when she talked real loud to me, when I tried to talk to her. Her hazel eyes had trouble focusing as she tried to keep them open when she spoke and slurred her speech. When she did speak, her breath smelled like the bar. She was always in a small group of men and women laughing and smoking cigarettes. When I came inside and tugged on her dress to talk to her, she pretended I wasn't there. When I did get her attention, she told me to go outside and play with the kids, or if I was hungry, go to Harry's and eat something.

This one day, while I was playing outside Harry's, all the kids were drawing on the sidewalk with big round pastel chalk we bought that afternoon at Harry's. We were all on our knees, drawing crazy pastel pictures of cats and dogs that looked more like cows and Picasso horses. As I drew quietly in the street, I lifted my head for a moment and I saw Mom leave the bar — she was headed in my direction. She didn't look quite right. She was stumbling as she walked, like her shoes were too big for her feet. Her face looked tight and her eyes were squinting like she couldn't take the sunlight, but she never took her eyes off me as she walked in my direction. Her teeth were clenched and her fists tight in a ball, rigidly by her side. As she marched toward me, my first mistake was to stand up and wait for Mom to arrive. At that moment, Mom unleashed a powerful right hook to the side of my head; it was shot forcibly to the opposite side from the force of the blow. Then her left fist hit me, knocking my head again to the other side.

With the precision of a prize fighter, she threw another punch, and her right hand connected with my jaw. Mom delivered a perfect right, left, right punch combination within what felt like a fraction of a second. I was out cold; I felt nothing. I had never been unconscious before — I heard ringing in my ears that was deafening. Being knocked out was nothing like I thought it would be. In the cartoons when Bluto knocked out Popeye, his eyes had big X's on them and blackbirds flew around his head in a circle, and a cuckoo clock sound filled his ears. Then Olive Oyl reached into Popeye's pocket and pulled out a can of spinach and put some in his mouth. As he chewed the spinach, Popeye's theme song played and Popeye came alive. His biceps had a picture of a tank on them as he flexed. His fists took the shape of hammers and Bluto took a beating from Popeye's twister punches. With one final punch, Bluto would fly through the air and wind up in the baby carriage with a bottle in his mouth and baby hat on, crying .Then Popeye and Olive Oyl, began to sing "He's Popeye the sailor man..." as they pushed Bluto in the baby carriage. Well.... That's not how it goes. There were no birds, no Olive Oyl, no spinach, and no theme song. It wasn't Bluto who knocked me out, it was Mom.

As I lay there unconscious, I felt warm drops of water on my face, followed by cold water splashing me from above. As I starting coming out of this sleep-like confusion, I looked up to see my mother. She was upside down, cradling me in between her legs; my head was on her lap as she sat Indian-style. Her warm tears were what I felt when I was out, and the cold water was being splashed on my face to help me regain consciousness. Florence, Harry's wife, came out from the candy store to help. It felt like I was out a long time, but after a few minutes, I was alive again! I was awake. I felt tired and drained, and Mom was noticeably shaken up. She was hugging me and kissing me as if it wasn't her who minutes ago executed a perfect three-punch knockout on her seven-year-old. I stood up on real wobbly legs, and Mom had her arm around me, trying to steady me as she walked me into Harry's candy store. There was a small crowd around me, just staring at the two of us.

Within minutes, as I sat on the stool at the counter, a bowl of ice cream in a small silver dish arrived. Mom's arm never left my shoulder as she continued to wipe my face clean from the crying marks that streaked down my cheeks. On the way out of Harry's she told me not to tell my father what happened. She bought me a yo-yo and a model airplane — what a small to price to pay for my silence, and such a great knockout.

That's Good Wine

IN MY APARTMENT on Morris Park Avenue in The Bronx, in the kitchen there was a small door. It was about three feet off the floor in the middle of the wall. It had a flip-over lock on it, and layers of paint that sealed it and kept it shut tight. My father explained to me that years ago when the building was new and you had garbage to throw out, you would ring the bell on the wall next to the door and the building's superintendent (super) would send up what looked like a small elevator. You would then open up the door, place your garbage in it, then shut the door and ring the bell. Then the super, through a series of ropes and pulleys, would take down the garbage to the basement to be collected and thrown out. This garbage elevator had a strange name — Dad called it a "dumbwaiter."

This garbage collection system with the dumbwaiter had long been out of use. It sounded like a good idea, but I never saw how it really worked. So all the apartments had this ugly useless door in the kitchen that did nothing and went nowhere. This door, even though it was closed, had a space big enough that cockroaches and water bugs would come into the apartment, from the basement and the apartments above and below us, all over the building. This dumbwaiter shaft was kind of an insect highway, where cockroaches could travel without getting stepped on by an angry shoe. It had all the makings of a great hideout, if you were a cockroach. No lights came on in the shaft, so they didn't have to scatter for cover — these are lucky roaches who traveled by the dumbwaiter highway.

Sometimes during the day when Mom wasn't out or sleeping, she would drink with the super, John Bruno. No one called him John; we all called him by his last name. Bruno was an older man, about the same age as my granddad. He was short and chubby. He had no teeth, but he had a great gummy smile like a baby, which made you like him instantly. I'm sure he enjoyed drinking with an attractive woman half his age (like my mom) whose husband was at work. My mother could get Bruno to fix anything, and after he fixed a leaky faucet that took only five minutes, they would drink for hours — or at least until Dad got home. Since the apartment always needed a little fixing, and they both liked a little drinking, Bruno was a frequent visitor.

Somehow, Mom talked Bruno into covering up the old ugly dumbwaiter with a sheet of wood and three poorly constructed wood shelves. For a Bronx apartment, this was a major renovation. Even though it wasn't perfect, it did seal up the dumbwaiter and made the kitchen look much better. The three empty shelves didn't remain empty for too long. My mother put three small bottles of cooking wine on each shelf. Anything you did to those small apartments was a major improvement since they all looked the same; they were dark and boxy like a railroad car.

It was a policy with the neighborhood kids that when it rained after school, we would watch TV together until our parents came home. This one afternoon, it was raining, so we couldn't play outside on the block. The four of us, me, Paulie, Kevin, and Carlo went up to my apartment to watch TV. After an hour of sitting on the couch and watching TV, Paulie went home. A half-hour later, Kevin went home. Now it was just me and Carlo watching TV. Carlo was a few years older than me, and he was the nephew of Eleanor, one of my mom's drinking buddies. He was also Roy's uncle. Everybody knew everybody on the block, so we were all together a lot. Even though Carlo was older than me, he acted about my age, and when we played sports, he was at the same skill level as me, since he was clumsy and a little bit slow — at least, that's what everybody said about Carlo.

We sat and watched TV for a while until Carlo said he was thirsty and he wanted a soda from the fridge. When he came back, instead of soda, he had a bottle of Mom's cooking wine. He was laughing so hard that he was doubled over, like he got punched in the stomach. I knew he was up to something — I'd seen that look before. He laughed and said, "Let's drink all the wine and get drunk like our mothers." With that being said, it was like we got the go-ahead, let's do it. He gave me a bottle, and his was already open as he gulped down the wine. After each sip he said, "That's good wine," in a deep voice, like he knew what good wine tasted like.

I twisted off the top of my bottle of wine, and put it to my lips. I sipped it, thinking, *Boy, is this wrong. Kids shouldn't be drinking. Drinking is for parents or adults.* With my first sip, I knew I didn't want another. It tasted like salad dressing, like vinegar. How could Carlo like this, and think it tasted good? I gave my bottle to Carlo, and I got a soda. We watched TV and with time, Carlo drank wine bottle after wine bottle. I'm not sure if he really liked the taste, or if he felt like an adult, but all he repeated was "That's good wine." After each bottle, Carlo told me how drunk he was getting, and he didn't care if we got caught; it was worth it to be drunk, he said. Carlo had convinced himself that he was drunk, and he was starting to slur his words just like my mom did. As he spoke, his eyes got heavy, and often they stayed closed too long like he was nodding to sleep. After drinking all nine of the small bottles of wine, Carlo slipped off the couch and onto the floor, and fell asleep. I was wide awake, still on my first Coke, watching TV. I watched Carlo "the drunk "sleep, and I wondered how this was going to end. Would my mother walk in, or would my father come home and see Carlo sleeping on the floor and the wine bottles all empty?

After all my favorite TV shows were over, it was getting late and I had to go to school tomorrow. I shut off the TV and tried to wake up Carlo so he could go home. As I spoke and pushed him to wake up, his eyes and voice responded slowly, just like Mom's when she was drunk. I helped him up off the floor; his legs were wobbly and he bumped into the wooden table in front of the couch — the same table that my dad and his friends thought was a stage on weekends, and would stand on and sing. He said he felt sick and didn't think he could make it home without throwing up. He had his arm around me for support as he walked.

We left the apartment and went down the hall to the elevator. As we walked, he told me the hallway was moving, as he took each step real slow so he wouldn't fall down. He walked like he was on ice skates.The elevator door opened. He sort of walked in and I sort of pushed him in as he propped his body up against the inside of the elevator. I reached over and pushed the lobby button, and the elevator door shut with Carlo still leaning against the side, trying to stay standing. I got two steps back to the apartment before I heard Carlo shout, "That's good wine."

When I got to the apartment, I put the wine bottles in the garbage and went to bed without eating any dinner, since nobody was home and it was too late to go to Harry's. I also didn't want to be awake just in case someone did come home and start to ask questions. I fell asleep and no one woke me. It was not unusual for no one to be home when I went to bed. No one tucked me in, and kissed me on the cheek, like in *Leave It to Beaver*.

In the morning when I woke up, I looked over to the other bed, as I shared the room with my parents. Dad was gone and Mom was snoring loudly with her eyes half closed; I knew nothing would wake her. I did what I did every morning, and then I went to school. When I got off the school bus, I walked down Morris Park Avenue. I knew I had to pass the bar on the way home. My mother was in the bar drinking with Eleanor, Carlos' aunt. My mother saw me and signaled with her hand to come over to her. I hoped she hadn't noticed the wine bottles were gone and in the garbage. I didn't want her to slap me in front of the people in the bar, or yell at me. She and Eleanor were both on their way to being drunk themselves. Judging by the time of day and the time they woke up, they had been drinking only for about an hour or two.

Eleanor put down her drink and kissed me on the cheek and said,

HEY...I'M JUST A KID

"You and Carlo were drinking last night." She laughed, stood up, and said, "How can you get drunk from cooking wine? When you get a little older, we'll show you how to drink."

She and my mom laughed, and the smell of alcohol and cigarettes was on my cheek from where she kissed me. Instead of being punished, it was all a big joke and a promise to show us later, when we got big, how to really drink. I told my mother I was hungry and I wanted to go to Harry's to get something to eat. All she said was "That's good," as she rocked back and forth, sipping her drink. So I left the bar with the two of them still laughing. They laughed with a drink in one hand and a cigarette in the other. No harm done last night. In my neighborhood nobody got punished, especially with parents like mine. I saw Johnny Moon standing outside the door in front of Harry's; I said his name and nodded my head in respect as I entered the candy store. I jumped up on the red stool and ordered a large chocolate egg cream, burger, and fries. Just another day in my neighborhood in The Bronx.

Mark's Bike

IT WAS A hot, muggy July day. Mark and I played in the shade provided by our six-story apartment building on Morris Park Avenue in The Bronx. Our bikes were out alongside the building while we wrote on the sidewalk with pastel chalk. Every few minutes, Mark glanced over at his bike. It was new. It was a 24-inch red Schwinn with chrome fenders and whitewall tires. It was magnificent — every boy's dream. Most of us had old hand-me-down bikes from older brothers, or we still had the bikes that were new three years ago. Now they were rusted, tires bald, seats torn. All of us, but not Mark. Mark always got a new bike every summer. Mark's family had a nice car, and he had the new bike. We were working-class poor, but we didn't know it; we all lived in the same neighborhood, and no one seemed to have more than anyone else, except Mark.

As we scribbled on the sidewalk, soon Mark and I were joined by two boys. These were new boys – boys we didn't know, and had never seen on our block before ... and we knew everybody. The new boys were black boys. Our neighborhood was Tremont and Morris Park Avenues, and up Tremont Avenue there were other neighborhoods with kids we didn't know. We were not allowed to leave our block. I'm seven and those are the rules.

With our new friends, we laughed and played for hours. We gave our new friends chalk and we wrote on the sidewalks and drew pictures. We played catch with our pink Spaldeen (Bronx for Spalding). We played box ball and hit the penny. We went to Harry's candy store, and we shared our lunch with our new pals, with our bikes parked out in front, so we could see them. The other boys' bikes were just like mine, old and rusted. As we ate, our bikes were on the ground — but not Mark's; his was upright on a kickstand. Mark's bike was so beautiful and new.

Like all boys, we liked to race around the block to see whose bike was the fastest. Having the fastest bike on the block really meant something. We finished eating and on the way out we all took whistle lollipops and went out to ride our bikes — all of us: me, Mark, and our new friends. Full of food and energy, we all rode our bikes around the block, each of us trying to ride the fastest and be out in front. Mark, after two times around the block, beat us all. Did he win because he had the best bike? Did he win because he was the best rider? Or did he win because he had the strongest legs?

We all pulled our bikes over, and Mark challenged all of us to a race. The corners at the end of every block were narrow and hard to turn on while going fast, so Mark said he'd race us one by one. Since Mark and I were long-time buddies, he challenged me first. Our new friends yelled, "On your marks, get set, go!" Mark and I took off. He took an early lead, and I never caught up to him. He beat me easily by a quarter of a block. Next up, he raced one of our new friends, and again, an easy win. Only one of us left to race, and Mark would become the fastest, best biker on Lebanon Street. The last boy got on his old bike and raced Mark. Once again, Mark was the winner. Like all winners, he gloated and said he was the best, the fastest, strongest rider on the block.

One of our new friends called out "do over." In The Bronx, at our age, "do over" means you didn't accept what just happened. It means "Let's do it again." Then, and only then, you were the real champion. One of our new friends told Mark, "You always win, but it's not you — you aren't stronger or a better biker; it's because we're on junk bikes, and it's the bike that's better, not you. I bet you can't beat me on my bike if I ride yours."

Mark had a swelled head by now; he beat all of us all day, every race. He accepted the kid's challenge and said, "It's not the bike, it's me. I don't care what I ride, I'm better than you." With that, Mark added, "I'll show you — you ride my bike, I'll ride your bike, and I'll still win." Mark jumped on the kid's old bike, and the other boy jumped on Mark's bike, and they lined up to race. The rules were that the first one around the block and back to the starting spot was the winner.

"On your marks, get set, go!" Mark and the boy took off, pedaling as fast as they could. Halfway down the block, Mark was far ahead in the lead. So, maybe he *was* the fastest biker. He made the turn at the corner, and we could no longer see him. He was on his way around the block to claim his victory. The other boy approached the turn, but he didn't slow down; he kept going straight until we could no longer see him. Within a few minutes, Mark circled the corner to where we were standing. He knew no one had passed him, so he yelled, "I won, I won, and I told you I'm the best." Mark jumped off the old bike, and we waited a few minutes. Mark said, "Where is that kid with my new bike?"

The other boy walked slowly to his bike; as he swung his leg over the bike and put his feet on the pedals, he looked calmly at us and said, "I'm going to go look for him — I hope he's okay and didn't fall down." He pedaled down the block and where he should have turned, at the corner, he hopped the curb and went into the street, and kept going straight. Mark and I looked at each other, not knowing what had just happened. We waited about five minutes, even though it felt like forever.

Our new friends never came back. Neither did Mark's bike. The two boys didn't want to play. They didn't want to make new friends; they wanted a new bike, and their plan worked perfectly. For the rest of that summer, Mark never bragged about anything anymore. He couldn't — the old rusted bike left behind was his now. That day I learned that when someone wants to be your friend, it may be more than just friendship they're looking for, and that day ... it was a beautiful new Schwinn bike.

Two Twenties

AN ENTIRE DAY could go by and not once did I see Mom, unless I looked for her. She was easy to find, and I knew where to look. Her life could have been a country song; she was either "sleeping, stealing, or drinking." I knew that if she wasn't upstairs at the apartment sleeping, and she was finished stealing — or as she called it, "going shopping" — sooner or later she would wind up at the bar on Morris Park Avenue next to Harry's candy store and Dunright movers. During the day, me and the other kids just drifted from Harry's candy store to the lots on Lebanon Street to play stickball and box ball.

Today, my friend of choice was Donald. We never called him Don or Donnie; he was always Donald. He told us he came from an Irish Catholic family and none of the kids were allowed to shorten or change their Christian given names. Donald went to Catholic school, unlike all of us who went to public school. He had better manners than we did, and had to be home at certain times, unlike the rest of us kids. Everybody on the block called him Donald, even though it sounded so formal, as if he wasn't really one of us. Most of us shortened our names or added a "ie" or a "y," so I became Ronnie, Paul became Paulie, and Anthony became Tony? "Donald" sounded more like a kid you really didn't know who sat behind you in school, but he was one of us.

We walked down Lebanon Street into the lots to look for old baby carriages. Donald was a build-it type of kid. He liked taking his father's tools and building things that we found in the lots. Sometimes it was wood and junk, tin and cardboard, but today Donald wanted to build a pushcart out of wood and carriage wheels. We looked in the lots for the wood and wheels we knew if we could find it Donald could build it, and I would help. Building a pushcart was something the boys in the neighborhood took pride in. It was always a lot of fun to build and ride, since two kids were needed. One kid would steer, and the other kid would push with his feet hanging off the back of the cart as we sat in the cart back-to- back. We could do this all day, and with few hills it could be exciting and not so exhausting if we could roll downhill a bit. Being a pusher was also rough on your sneakers, since you were also the brake man. The only way to stop was to put your feet down on the concrete and burn rubber — real tough on my high top Converse sneakers.

As we searched the lots to make our *Flintstones* leg-powered pushcart, I saw two green crumpled pieces of paper on the gravel-covered ground near a puddle. Since the lots were never cared for, the ground was not level, and there were puddles that seemed never to evaporate. A small breeze came through the lots. The two green pieces of paper danced on the ground as they caught my eye again. They were money! Now I clearly saw the size and shape of the green paper. Before it blew away in the wind, or Donald saw it — it was mine. I ran toward the bills and started yelling, "Finders keepers, losers weepers!" over and over until it was in my hand. That's how you staked a claim in The Bronx. By the time it took Donald to raise his head up to see what I was yelling about, I had two twenty-dollar bills in my hands.

I'd never seen a twenty-dollar bill before, and now I had two of them. They looked like dollar bills, but they had the number twenty in the corners, and the old guy in the middle of the bill looked different. I thought to myself, *I'm rich now. I can have anything I want, and everything I want is at Harry's candy store.* Behind the glass showcase in the back of Harry's there were real toys. Not just balls and cap guns and wood assembly airplanes, but real toys. Expensive toys. Big trucks, cars, train sets, a microscope with butterfly slides — the list of great toys went on and on.

As Donald ran over to me to look at the two twenty-dollar bills, I told him that even though I was the finder in finders keepers, I'd buy him something at Harry's candy store, and he could share in my fortune. We walked out of the lots like two California gold rush miners who were going to Harry's to buy up the town. We sat at the counter on the red leather stools and I told Florence, Harry's wife, about the money I found. She smiled and poured us Cokes like Kitty in *Gunsmoke* poured whiskey at her tavern. I told Florence to put on burgers and fries, and when we were done, we'd be getting some toys from the glass showcase in back of the store. I told her we both wanted toys — me and Donald. We were going to see just how much two twenty-dollar bills could get us.

As the burgers and fries cooked up, me and Donald got off the stools and eyeballed the toys behind the glass. Normally they were off our toy menu, but today we were window shopping for some serious toys. I liked the fire truck with the plastic ladder that opened up to three feet long, and squirted water through the hose when you pumped it. Donald had his eye on a big green plastic airplane that dropped plastic bombs through a chute as you held it and pretended to fly. In the middle of this fantasy, we heard a voice calling us: "Boys, boys ... you're up, you're up," said Florence.

We climbed back on the stools and dug into the burgers and fries like we hadn't eaten in days. When you have money in your pocket, everything just feels different. Even the burgers were better. We were eating faster than usual; we knew the sooner we finished, the sooner we could get to the toys, and be on the street playing with them.

Just then, I heard a voice that I had not heard all day. "Ronnie, Ronnie — come here; I want to talk to you." It was Mom. My mother hardly talked to me, so I knew this couldn't be good, especially since I was holding two twenty-dollar bills in my pocket, and I already had them spent. Her voice was stern when she spoke to me, like I did something wrong. She said, "I heard you found forty dollars, and you have to give it back. It was mine; I lost it, so give it back." She put out her hand and waited for me to go into my pocket to give her the money I found. She stood in front of me and rocked a little bit back and forth, and I smelled the bar on her breath, so I knew she was drinking next door. That's how she knew about the money!!! She didn't lose it; somebody from Harry's must have heard me talking to Florence and went next door and told Mom.

I reached into my pocket and gave Mom the two twenty-dollar bills, since she looked like she wasn't going to leave without them. I didn't want to give the money to her. What I wanted to do was call her a liar. I knew there was no way she could've lost the money and I just happened to find it two blocks away near a puddle in the lots. But what was I to do? As I handed her the money she said, "Good boy, and don't tell your father." She walked out of Harry's and made a left and went back into the bar. Me and Donald just looked at each other. We both knew the toys behind the glass were going to stay on the shelf and not be ours. My fortune — our fortune — was gone.

I told Florence that I had no more money, and to put our lunch on my dad's tab, and he'd pay Harry on Friday. She put her head down and walked over to a notebook. She said, "Tell your father he's up to twenty two dollars, plus whatever he owes Harry — and you guys ate another three dollars and sixty-five cents."

Me and Donald walked out of the candy store; he looked at me and said, "At least we got to eat." I didn't know what to say, so I said nothing. I walked a few steps over, in front of the bar. I saw Mom on the barstool with Eleanor, and next to them were my two twenty-dollar bills on the bar. So even though I called "finders keepers." The finder-me-didn't get to keep it;The keeper was Mom. I thought to myself, *The next time I find anything, I'm going to sneak it into my pocket quietly without telling anyone, and remember what just happened. If there is a next time, no one, not even Donald, will know.*

Nanny used to say, "Good news travels fast." But today, the news of my two twenties reached my mom before I even finished my hamburger.

Blood in the Snow

THIS WAS THE third time we went upstate to Margaretville to visit Uncle Funzy and his family. It was a cold, snowy winter day. I made a fort in the back of Dad's old '57 Chevy that he called "The Silver Bullet." I was surrounded by blankets and pillows to keep me warm and comfortable. Dad was driving, and Mom was in the front seat next to him, wrapped in two blankets. It was cold in the car, and the heater didn't work very well. When the warmth of our breath frosted the windshield, Dad pushed in the cigarette lighter; when it got hot and popped out, he dragged it across the windshield to help melt the frost so he could see better. Since the radio didn't play well once we left The Bronx, it was a long, quiet ride. After a few hours of driving, we got off the highway and into the town of Margaretville, my dad said to look for Dry Brook Road. That day nothing was dry and I couldn't see a brook – just mountains of uncleared snow and barely visible roads.

After a mile or two of driving slow and getting stuck in the snow, we saw their house. They must have been waiting for us. As soon as the car stopped and we opened our doors, they were standing there. We smiled and laughed and hugged each other as we made our way toward the house. There was no walk path, and the snow was as high as their front windows. The house was slightly warmer than the car, so we kept our jackets on as we stood in the kitchen. It was strange to see Uncle Funzy as a family man. Whenever I saw him, he was alone and covered in paint, sleeping on our couch. If he got in early enough, we ate together as he painted on blank canvases while I sat on the floor next to him, watching him turn them into fine art.

The oven door was open, throwing out heat, even though they weren't cooking. The top burners were on, with water boiling in big black pots — anything to make the house warmer. In the next room there was a fireplace that was roaring full blast in a losing battle to heat the cold, damp room. I hadn't seen Uncle Funzy's family since the summer. Seeing them again reminded me of how much I missed them. His wife was Dolores, who possessed stunning good looks and a shy "brought up in the country" demeanor. They had two kids — a girl, Rosie, a cute, chubby blonde-haired girl with red cheeks and a dirty face; and Frankie, a tall thin boy with black hair. Frankie was about my age.

Their house was big and cold, so we kept our clothes on with sweaters under our jackets to keep warm. There was something nice about sitting together in the kitchen while we all ate and talked during dinner. Funzy's familiar hyena laugh filled the room as Dolores smiled shyly. They were like the families who live in the country I saw on television. Not an ounce of "come from the city" in this family. As I looked around, I realized how different their lives were from mine. There were no other houses or people around for miles. Where I lived, in one apartment building, there were probably more people than in all of Margaretville. Outside their house there were enough trees to call it a forest. My forest was other apartment buildings standing side-by-side that huddled together, keeping the sun out. My forest was concrete and bricks — after all, I was a city kid.

After dinner, me, Frankie, and Rosie went out the front door and made a snowman and threw a few snowballs until our hands burned with frozen fingers through our soaked wool gloves. That night, Me, Frankie and Rosie slept in the same bed after we had hot chocolate and cookies in the warm kitchen. We huddled together with blankets and overcoats on top of the blankets to help keep us warm. When it was this cold, we slept under the covers without moving, like mummies. Getting out of bed to pee during the night wasn't an option until the morning.

The cold night and warm clothing made for great sleep. We woke up early at sunrise, all three of us. Soon, with us laughing and giggling, the house came alive with the adults who were now awake. Dolores made a big breakfast in the kitchen that had the stove on all night for heat. She made the best scrambled eggs I ever ate. She said the secret to the eggs was that she put in American cheese and it all melted together. As soon as the last mouthful was chewed, we ran outside to play in the snow. It was easy, since we were already dressed from yesterday.

Once outside, there were four deer just a few feet from the house. With the noise of the closing door, for a moment they lifted their heads up and looked straight at us. Frankie and Rosie weren't excited like I was. They saw deer all the time, but I couldn't take my eyes off them. I never saw real deer before. They were bigger than I thought, and against the white snow they looked darker than I thought. They had big brown eyes that were the size of marbles, and long pointed ears, pointed in our direction, listening to us. To our left there were bare trees that looked like big skeletons since they had no leaves. There were small black sparrows everywhere in the trees, flying back and forth from one branch to another. There were so many of these black sparrows that their chirping filled the quiet mountain air. Living in the country is different from living in the city.

Frankie said, "Hear that?" That's a gunshot — somebody's hunting. We do a lot of hunting up here. We hunt deer and rabbits and raccoons. I even hunt birds."

Even though I knew about hunting, I never saw it done and I never did it. In the city where I lived, nobody carried guns and nobody hunted. Frankie said he loved hunting, and he had a BB rifle that shot small pellets. We walked over to the side of the house and walked into a small shed where they kept firewood. Leaning against the side near the door was Frankie's BB rifle. He took the rifle in his right hand and the back of it was in his armpit, just like I saw on television. He looked like a real hunter, only smaller. Whenever he saw something move, he lifted the rifle to his shoulder and tilted his head down on it to look down the gun barrel. After he aimed, he shot. The shooting didn't make a lot of noise like the hunters' guns we heard from far away. He shot at anything and everything. After each shot, he pumped the handle to ready another BB.

We walked over to the tree with all the birds that were chirping. Frankie lifted the rifle and started shooting at the birds as they flew back and forth chirping from branch to branch. He shot and pumped and pointed the rifle at the trees with the birds in it, over and over again. He looked like he was having so much fun and acting so grown-up to be able to hunt. He said, "All men up here hunt." After every shot he took, he said it again: "All men up here hunt." I wanted to feel what he felt. I wanted to be a hunter too, like Frankie.

I'd never shot a BB rifle before, and I knew it was dangerous, so I went into the house and asked Uncle Funzy if I could try Frankie's gun. He smiled and said, "Just make sure you don't shoot at each other," as he laughed and shook his head.

I went back outside to Frankie and told him that his dad gave me permission to try the BB gun. Frankie passed me the rifle without hesitation with a big smile on his face, like we were sharing manhood together. Now we would both be hunters. He showed me how to aim, shoot, press the lever down, and squeeze the trigger. After a few shots, I felt so powerful and grown-up to be hunting and shooting a gun. Now I knew what Frankie felt when he was talking to me before and smiling while he pulled the trigger on the rifle.

The birds in the trees chirped so loud, they caught my attention. We went under the tree and began shooting at the birds. I aimed, I fired, I aimed and fired, and nothing. Not one bird. Frankie said, "Take aim, boy — take your time and keep shooting; you'll get one."

I shot a few more times, and then something happened. One of the BB pellets made contact with a bird as it flew from branch to branch. Its wings flapped frantically as it fell from the tree into the snow. As the bird hit the snow, Frankie screamed, "You got 'em, you got 'em." I knew I didn't know how to aim; the bird must've flown into the BB pellet at the exact moment of the shot.

As the small black bird fluttered around in a circle, red blood droplets stained the pure white snow from where it was hit. Seeing the bird hurt and bleeding, I started to cry. I knew I had done something wrong. It didn't feel the way I thought it would, being a hunter, being a man with a gun. I was a boy crying, and Frankie was laughing at me. He said, "What did you think was going to happen when you shot it?" I couldn't answer, because I never shot anything before. I really didn't know what was supposed to happen. It wasn't a good feeling. Why did I follow Frankie and his hunting and shooting? I thought city kids were tougher than the country kids. So why was I crying uncontrollably?

I kept looking down at the little black bird in the snow, bleeding with its wings flapping, no longer up in the tree with the other birds, singing and flying from branch to branch. The bird flapped its wings for a few minutes that felt more like a few hours. I stood there crying until the bird stopped moving. I fell to my knees and picked it up in my hands, still crying. Over and over I said, "I'm sorry, I'm so sorry, I didn't know this would happen. I never wanted to hurt you."

All the while, Frankie was pointing at me laughing. He called me a girl and told me, "Stop talking to a dead bird and go inside with my sister Rosie where you belong, and play with dolls."

On Lebanon Street, if someone said that to me, I would have punched him and fought him, to show him how tough I really was. Instead, I handed Frankie back the gun slowly, not caring what he said to me. I asked him to help me bury the bird. He told me to leave it in the snow — some animal would come along and eat it tonight — but I couldn't. I got a stick and dug through the snow until I found dirt. I made a small hole and placed the dead bird in the hole, and covered it back with the dirt. I never stopped crying while all this was going on, and Frankie never stopped laughing at me for crying. He said, "It's only a bird; look how many more there are in that tree."

At that moment, I hated him for saying that. It made the bird's life so unimportant. What I did was so unforgivable. Even though I'm just a kid, I should have known better. I didn't know what I did, until I did it. I'm only nine years old, but I know I'll never be a hunter when I grow up. Birds belong in trees...not dead and buried in the ground.

Little League

THE WINTER'S COLD was gone now. The trees across the street near the bus stop were starting to sprout the buds that magically grow leaves in the summer. The brown grass under the tree was changing color, too — from straw yellow to dark green, like a baseball field. Spring was here, and in the spring every boy dreams of baseball. It's just the thing we do. It's one of the things a kid my age waits for, as the weather gets warmer.

A few blocks from the apartment buildings that surrounded me was a neighborhood in The Bronx we called "Van Nest." This neighborhood had private homes with concrete steps and iron gates around them. They weren't big or fancy, but compared to an apartment building, they were. The "Van Nest" neighborhood had a real baseball field. It looked like the baseball fields on television — only smaller, and surrounded by chain-link fencing. It had a home plate, first base, second base, and third base. On the sides of the field, there were wooden benches to sit on that started out at ground level and went up a dozen rows for people to watch the games.

The day I went there, there were two grown men with baseball hats and Yankee jackets on. They had equipment bags with baseball bats and gloves that they were handing out. It looked like they were going to play a game, so I stood in line with the other boys. After all, this was a real baseball diamond, and grown-ups were around to supervise. One of the men gave me a glove and told me to "stand out there, stand out there," as he pointed. He pointed to the outfield.

I ran to the outfield, and within a few minutes these men pointed all the boys to a position on the field. When they were done, I looked around, and smiled to myself — we sure looked like a baseball team. It was different from the field I played on. Home plate wasn't a sewer and first base wasn't a car door handle. Second base was a real base, and third base was a real third base, not a car on the other side of the street.

The two men took to the field, too. One was at bat, and one was on the field yelling out to us what to do. A few balls were hit to me on the ground, and the baseball man shouted, "Throw to first, throw to first." Which I did. As soon as I threw it, the man yelled, "Nice arm, kid — nice arm, kid!" I was glad he thought it was a nice arm; the other one had a glove on it and couldn't throw a ball.

As the batting baseball guy continued to hit the ball, one pop fly was coming in my direction. The same baseball guy who liked my arm pointed to me and shouted, "Pop fly, pop fly, get under it, get under it!" Which I did. I caught it easily without dropping the ball like most of the other boys. As I caught the ball, the baseball man said, "Good glove, good glove." For some reason, the baseball guy said everything twice, and loud, in a strong voice, as he chewed gum and spit a lot from the side of his mouth.

After I caught a few more balls, he pointed to me and told me, "Get up at bat, get up at bat." He pitched the ball to me slow and underhand, not like on television. I easily connected with every pitch he tossed, as he yelled, "Nice shot, nice shot!" After everybody got a turn at bat, he waved his arms and shouted to come in. He meant the game was over. We all crowded around the two baseball guys. I was having such a good time; I was sorry to see it end. He instructed us to put the gloves in the big green duffel bag, and pick up the baseball bats and balls and do the same. I was walking over to say thanks for letting me play, but before I got there, in a loud voice, loud enough so we all could all hear, he said, "Okay — I'll see you guys tomorrow; same time, and same field."

What a great afternoon I had, playing real baseball with kids and gloves and grown-up baseball guys to guide us. It was a lot different from the stickball that I played, and from what I was used to. The next day after school I went to the Van Nest neighborhood, and went on the field to play again. We did the same things we did yesterday, but today it was even more fun, since I got friendly with some teammates. At the end of the game, the baseball guys handed out papers and told us to have our parents sign the bottom, and bring it back with twenty-five dollars for the Little League. He said, "You will all get uniforms next week."

After he said this, I knew that this would be the last time I got to play at Van Nest. I knew I couldn't come back with the signature and money to play on the Little League. I didn't have those kinds of parents. I had the kind of parents that never had money and they charged everything around the neighborhood. I wasn't in my own neighborhood now. Here, they didn't know my parents and I couldn't charge anything. The signature part wouldn't be easy, either. My mother was always sleeping or at the bar, so to approach her to sign something probably wouldn't go too well. As for the money, I usually saw my dad at night after he came home from work, but I didn't think I should ask him for twenty-five dollars, when he had to charge everything at Harry's candy store, and Bernie's grocery store. I didn't think he carried that kind of money with him. Maybe on Friday —that was payday — but even on Friday, when he got off the train, he paid Harry and Bernie before he came up to the apartment. By the time he got to me, I knew he wouldn't have much money left. Even if I could get the money somewhere, the last time I asked to have something signed from the school, it remained on the kitchen table until it wasn't necessary anymore and eventually wound up in the garbage.

The other kids also had parents who came with them to the practices and to the games. They sat on the side on the wooden benches, to cheer their kids on for encouragement. How could I bring my mother to the game? If she wasn't at the bar or upstairs sleeping, she would never walk me to the baseball field, and stay there to watch me. Dad would've been a good baseball candidate for me, but during the week he worked, and didn't come home until five or six o'clock. On Saturdays and Sundays he was out at the racetrack, or had his friends come over to sing to the doo-wop records they played, or they played chess while they smoked thin stinky cigarettes. It looked as if my playing real baseball with a team would be impossible, since it wasn't for kids like me.

I didn't even have a baseball glove, but that problem, I knew I could solve. I could make friends with the boys on the other team. While they were up at bat, I could borrow a glove to play the field with, and switch with them when it was my turn to bat. Most of the other kids got driven to play baseball, but I could walk to the field. So I got the glove covered, and the transportation covered, but the twenty-five dollars and the signature from a parent … those two things were going to be the "strike-out" of my baseball career. As I walked back to Lebanon Street, before I could think about missing baseball, I found a fairly new pink Spaldeen (Spalding) in the street next to a sewer. The writing was still on it, and I could barely squeeze it between my palm and fingers. This ball had plenty of bounce. Now I was thinking, *I'll go back to the neighborhood, and go to Harry's candy store and get some kids on the block to play ball.*

My kind of ball, stickball. After all, when one ball bounces out of your glove...you catch the next one with both hands.

Mom, What Are You Looking For?

I PUSHED OPEN the apartment door, which was never locked. I heard Mom crying in the bedroom as she talked to herself. "Where did it go, where did I leave it, I know it's it here." She was crying so hard that she didn't even notice me walk in. Even though I was right behind her, she didn't feel my presence. Most of the time, coming into the apartment, it was quiet and peaceful. She was either out at the bar for the afternoon, or sleeping in the bedroom. The same bedroom now looked like a hurricane blew through the apartment and scattered everything onto the floor. She was standing in front of her dresser, going through the drawers. After every drawer she opened, she felt around inside, and a moment later it was pulled from the dresser and dumped on the floor. Even though the drawer was upside down and empty, she continued to shake it, like she was waiting for something else to fall. After every drawer was emptied and on the floor, she got on her knees to look closer, as her hands and fingers explored the rubble. She never lifted her head up, or recognized I was in the room. As she stood up, tears streamed down her face and into her mouth. She picked up her underwear that was on the floor and wiped her face. I asked her "Mom, what are you looking for?"

Her head didn't turn toward me, and she didn't answer. It was like she never heard my voice. She opened the next drawer and followed the same pattern. Her hand went left, and then her hand went right as she tossed the items inside. Then she pulled out the drawer from the dresser, and dumped everything on the floor, as she continued to cry and look for something. I wanted to help her — if only she would tell me what she was looking for, I would get down on the ground and look with her. All her drawers were on the floor now; they were all pulled out of the dresser. She dove back on the floor like a hungry dog looking through garbage. She was crying and mumbling to herself, "I know it's here, I know it's here."

Once again I asked her, "What did you lose? I'll help you."

She turned her head slowly and snapped back at me as she clenched her teeth, "None of your business." She remained on the floor examining every article of clothing that was dumped there. I wondered to myself what she could be looking for. What could be so important that made her so upset to lose? Seeing her cry and mumble to herself made her look more like a sad little girl than a grown-up.

Even though I didn't know what I was looking for, I joined her on the floor. There we were, shoulder to shoulder, turning over under-wear and sweaters and socks. I looked like I knew what I was looking for, but I didn't. I just wanted to help her, by being there on the floor with her. Again I asked her, "Mom, I don't even know what I'm look-ing for."

She said, "Mommy is looking for pills. Ah, uh …. Vitamin pills and money I hid from your father."

I asked her, "Mom, why isn't your money in your pocket book, and vitamins in the kitchen drawer with the aspirins?" With her head down, looking frantically, pushing everything around, she looked like a miner panning for gold in a river. "Mom," I said "he doesn't know you have vitamins and money?"

She didn't answer me; she stopped what she was doing and gave me a familiar look. I'd seen that look before on her face, when she had been drinking too much … like the way a dog snarls right before it's about to bite. Her face got tight and she bit down on her teeth. She stood up, and smacked me in the face. I looked back at her, like her smack didn't hurt, even though it did. It wasn't my face that hurt — it was that I was helping her, and she didn't appreciate it. I no longer wanted to help her look for anything. I didn't care if she ever found what she was looking for, after that smack.

I left the apartment and took the staircase to go downstairs. I knew if I took the elevator, someone might be in it and see me crying, and I didn't want to be embarrassed. In front of her I didn't cry a tear. I didn't want to give her the satisfaction that she got me to cry. I wanted to show her that I didn't care enough about her to make me cry. As I was walking down the stairs, I wiped my eyes from the few tears I couldn't hold back. I only had a few flights of stairs to prepare myself to meet the kids playing outside the building. I had to forget what just happened upstairs with Mom. In my neighborhood, you don't let them see you cry. Only babies cry.... And I'm not a baby.

Back Page

WHEN THINKING BACK to when you were seven or eight or nine years old, before adult life kicks in, being a child is a happiest you will ever be. Your whole world is so small, with boundaries everywhere. Your happiest moments could be summed up by a good cartoon, or a small toy. What is so special about childhood is that it is temporary. Your childhood consciousness really ends at about ten years old, when you hit that puberty wall. Then you are an adult forever. That short period called childhood ends. The way you walked, talked, and all you were, ends. Like the caterpillar becomes a butterfly — the butterfly can't crawl on the ground anymore the way it once did. As an adult you will never feel like a child again, even though daily we all try to capture those simple moments of youthful careless bliss. There's a cast of characters and events that shaped you unconsciously. They stay with you in your memory, although you'll never be there, or see them again. In the end, you don't draw anything from your past — your past draws you.

CPSIA information can be obtained at www.ICGtesting.com
Printed in the USA
BVOW01s2357280414

351956BV00001B/119/P